MOTHER MAY I

With All Due Respect

*Addressing the Silent Wars Between
Mothers and Daughters*

LaKisha Hinton-Williams

ISBN: 979-8-9993193-3-3

Edited, Formatted and Published by Empower Her Publishing, LLC

empowerherpublishing.com

Dedication

My Husband, Matthew:

Our paths crossed three times. The first time was in elementary school in Baltimore, Maryland in 1978. Your family then moved to North Carolina, while mine also moved back to North Carolina as well. However, we didn't actually meet again until we both found ourselves in Virginia as adults in 2019, coincidentally at Ollie's, a discount store. Thank goodness we both love a good deal! I know God doesn't make mistakes, so I grabbed two packs of curtains to ask for your opinion on which one looked the best. The kids would say that I shot my shot! It was a hilarious moment we shall never forget and I thank God every day that it worked! I believe that He was preparing us all along for this reunion since our initial encounter.

Thank you for always supporting me, being the man of God that you are, and for leading our family with strength and poise, especially when I'm not at my best.

My Daughter, Nevaeh:

At 37, I found myself purchasing every baby book I could find, thinking that it would ease my fear and help me with this new bundle of joy. Your grandmother told me that the only book I needed was the Bible. For 15 years, I have been reading and teaching that same book to you. Never let anyone take or misuse what God has given to you.

Thank you for always saying yes when I ask if I sound like Mary J. Blige when attempting to sing, and for pretending to believe me when I claimed I was a member of Salt-N-Pepa. You knew I was exaggerating, but you played along with my little fantasy—that is, until the movie came out! We laughed so hard at my delusion. I thank God for allowing you to come into this world through me. You are beautiful, inside and out. Remember, change is okay; it is how you embrace it that matters. Lastly, ALWAYS MEANT IT!

My Dearest Mother:

Thank you for your strength and resilience, which you continually display. Your support and love have played a vital role in shaping the woman and mother I have become. I proudly dedicate this book to you as a testament to your influence, sacrifice, and your unconditional love. I am so blessed to have a mother who understood her assignment.

Finally, to all the wonderful women who thought enough of me to share some of the most intimate details of your lives: You will never know how much it means to me to be able to offer a project that will have such an impact to help heal broken hearts and break generational curses. I am eternally grateful.

TABLE OF CONTENTS

Preface

For as long as I can remember, I've been blessed with a large family — grandmothers, aunts, uncles, and 1,001 cousins — and my life was filled with love and laughter. We weren't "play play" cousins either; these were running-through-your-veins, blood relatives who enriched my childhood with endless adventures and heartfelt connections. Growing up, I often thought some of my aunties and uncles were rich rich, but the truth is, we were all rich in the kind of wealth that truly matters: family and love. Our celebrations ranged from family reunions, to cousin gatherings at Aunt Nita's house, and Uncle Ernest's unforgettable block parties. The joy of those moments!

We celebrated life by showering each other with love, sharing rolling-on-the-floor laughs, joking with each other about everything and nothing at all, shedding some tears, reconciling, and sleeping well, just to do it all over again the very next day.

During the holidays, our grandmother had her own special way of deciding when we would travel. She really wanted to stay home for most of them, but my mother and aunt always made other plans for her that involved hitting the road. They never listened to what she actually wanted to do. They thought they were doing what was best, right? Right.

My grandmother's passing marked a turning point for our family. It became painfully evident that, without her guiding presence, we began to lose the sense of harmony that once characterized our family. The hate, anger, and disarray grew within the family, and opened my eyes to a harsher truth: it wasn't just other families who faced turmoil; mine did as well.

In my quest for clarity and guidance, I started repeating a phrase my mother and grandmother always reassured me with: "It starts here, at home, with us." In my community, this sentiment mostly referred to a household with a dedicated single mother at home, raising her child or children to the best of her ability – much like my mother and grandmother had done. In some cases, resources were minimal; yet, a mother's love always surpassed anything we thought we wanted. Why? Because her love was consistent. That love, consistency, and wisdom continues to inspire my mission today.

The importance of such unwavering love hit me in a very personal way after reading a text message from a friend who confided in me about the struggles she was facing with her adult daughter. Recognizing the bond I share with my daughter, I could not fathom a world where my child felt unable to discuss her thoughts and feelings with me. If not me, then who would be there for her? Inevitably, I felt a sense of fulfillment in doing my part by surrounding her with God-fearing people who are invested in her well-being; but as her mother, I always want to be the first one she entrusts with life issues.

I had just dedicated my life to Christ when I began therapy and I asked God to forgive me of all my sins. We had just wrapped up a group session at church when my First Lady prayed over me and told me to forgive anyone who had wronged me. I interrupted that prayer with a nudge because I thought the devil was using her tongue! The first person I felt had wronged me was my Junior High School basketball coach who raped me. I never forgave him. So when my therapist recommended I write a letter to the source of my nightmares, of course he was the first person to get that pen to pad.

Some people think we should just get over it because it happened so long ago. I thought I did. I joined the Navy, reinvented myself, and tried to move away from everyone who knew. Ultimately, I became Chief Petty Officer, then became a mother to the most beautiful baby girl at the ripe old age of 37. Fast forward to retirement after 24 years in the Navy and this new life was a huge adjustment. I had not realized just how much that day and his actions had impacted my life—from the effect on my Naval career to ruined and strained relationships with family and friends. And awe hell nawl! It later affected my love life. I knew in my heart that if I allowed him to continue mentally controlling my life, I would keep damaging my relationship with my husband (I will save that tea for the sequel).

In light of this, I began to write more. One letter turned into a stack of letters, knowing I would never actually mail them. I did so much writing and releasing, I started to become frightened by the thought of someone actually reading my letters, my private thoughts. I've even considered the potential consequences should that situation arise. My therapist and I have been busy!

Over time, I developed a habit of rereading specific letters as needed, as though they were prescriptions. I didn't expect for one letter to initiate such a powerful journey. My second letter was to my mother and I didn't even know I needed to write it. I certainly wouldn't send it out of respect, as my relationship with my mom was perfect — or so I thought. My faith enabled me to initiate my healing process by reminding me of the power of *grace*, *forgiveness*, and *testimony*. Those three words were a constant ring in my ears. That is, until the day I received a letter from my own daughter confessing to me that she was gay. How many of you know that it hits a lot different when it comes from the seed that you nurtured for nine months?

By the way, my daughter's letter to me is included in this book, along with my letters to both my mother and daughter.

LaKisha Hinton-Williams

A mother and daughter

1,206 Seconds of New Energy

Life is filled with challenges, but when you are a child made to feel like it is your duty to be the woman of the house, it puts you in unfortunate survival mode. A daughter recalls the strength she has gained along her life's journey. Her narrative tells a powerful story of growth and survival, as well as the ongoing quest for understanding and fulfillment for herself, but also for her mother and daughter, and their relationship as a whole.

Dear Mama,

There's so much I've carried in my heart over the years – some things I've been too afraid to say out loud, and others I simply didn't know how to express. But today, I want to speak from a place of respect, love, honesty, and healing. I didn't realize it then, but growing up while facing the challenges of your mental health episodes shaped me in more ways than I can count. As I have reflected over the many years of my adult life, I saw the weights you carried and the silent internal battles you fought. Even as a child, I knew you were doing the best you could with the hand of cards life dealt you, but that didn't mean it didn't deeply hurt me. I felt lost, alone, and like I had to figure out how to mother myself – and far too early.

I vividly remember the days after Dad left us after you two had been married for 20 years. That is what ultimately led to the mental breakdowns. I was just a child, but suddenly, I became the one paying the bills. I was cashing checks, writing checks, juggling final notices, bathing and clothing you all while pretending to be strong while watching you sink deeper into sadness. I didn't yet know how to name depression, nor did I fully understand it, but I could feel the shift in our home. The silence, the heaviness, the absence – not just of Dad, but of you, too. Emotionally, you gave up on everything. Your life, and entire whole world, had been centered around Dad, and when he left, it all fell apart.

His departure etched a lasting lesson into my soul and would forever be a part of my existence. I made a quiet promise to myself that I would never let one person have that much power over me – not emotionally, spiritually, or physically. I've built a wall of strength, not because I didn't want love, but because I was afraid of losing myself inside of it and not loving the things that once gave me joy and peace. I became determined to survive on my own terms. I told myself I would never be a nobody, even if I didn't know who I truly was yet.

Ultimately, I became a mother myself as a teenager – not out of readiness, but out of a deep unmet need for love, stability, and connection. I craved something unshakable, something that wouldn't change overnight. While I would never trade my children for anything in this world, I can't deny how difficult it was to start that journey so young, unprepared, and lacking true love from my own mother. I've also navigated through two divorces and several relationships, each one representing another chapter in my search for something I never fully understood: trust, security, peace, and unconditional love. As I reflect, I never really learned how to build strong, lasting bonds outside of my children. Emotional intimacy felt foreign as I became an expert at surviving, but never quite being fully in relationships.

Despite all the pain that we endured during my childhood and adolescence, I need you to know this: you gave me more than you probably realize. Your strength – even when it came through brokenness – helped shape the resilience in me. Watching you struggle and still get up, even if slowly, even if not always fully, showed me what surviving looked like. You gave me fire. You gave me grit. You gave me the will to rise even when I had to do it alone. This letter isn't about blame; it's about release. It's about acknowledging where I've been and why. It's about allowing myself to feel all of it – the anger, the grief, the confusion, and yes, the gratitude, because in your darkest moments, you still taught me how to keep moving. Somehow, while drowning in the depths of your silence, I learned how to speak up for myself and others. In your struggles, I learned how to stand on my own, even while completely vulnerable at times.

I love you, Mom. I always have, I always will, and I hope that by writing this, we can begin to make peace with the past while still honoring the woman I've become.

With all my heart,

Your Baby Girl

"Instead, be kind to each other, tenderhearted, forgiving one another just as God through Christ has forgiven you." Ephesians 4:32 (KJV)

Reflections

Use this space to write a memory, letter, or personal reflection.

"Let us not become weary in doing good, for at the proper time we will reap a harvest if we do not give up." Galatians 6:9 (NIV)

My First Best Friend

What do you do when you fear the first man who is supposed to protect and love you? When you witness abuse and then become a victim yourself? The fear of abandonment can leave you silenced and confused about where to seek help. This letter conveys a daughter's struggle to understand her mother and the pain stemming from their past.

Dear Mama,

For as long as I could remember, you were my first best friend. From how you wore your hair to the nail polish you used to wear on your nails, I wanted to be like you. You encouraged me to be well-spoken, well-dressed, and to always be a lady. My early memories were happy, and I always wanted to be around you. But then something shifted. I didn't know that you were unhappy in your marriage to my father. I remember when you went from being a stay-at-home mom to a working mom. It meant being around you all of the time to just some of the time. During the times you were working, my brother and I would be alone with Daddy. He drank a lot and he was mean. I was scared of him.

One day, while you were gone, he came into the living room and grabbed me. He held on to me while plugging in the iron you used earlier that day to iron your uniform. I wasn't sure what he was about to do, but I remember trying to get away. He touched the iron to see how hot it was and it had gotten hot really fast. The next thing I knew, my dad had lifted my shirt and pressed the iron into my back. I screamed to the top of my lungs and then he put the iron down. Sobbing tears fell instantly. It hurt so bad! Callously, he went into the fridge and grabbed butter. It was the big tub of Country Crock butter that you would buy. He took this big glob of butter and started spreading it across my back. It smelled like something was cooking. He tried as best as he could to bandage me up, and told me I'd better tell you that I was running by the iron and it fell on my back when you returned home.

When you arrived later that evening, I ran into your arms faster than I ever have before. I couldn't lie to you. I told you the truth and Daddy tried to lie. To my utter disbelief, you didn't call the police or pack up my brother and me. You chose to stay. I got up the next morning and stood with my back to the mirror by our front door. I lifted the bandages and saw the center of my back where my skin used to be. I was seven years old. I was a kid. You were not there to protect me from him. I had to wear multiple shirts under my school shirt to hide the impression of the bandages on my back. I guess we eventually ran out of the correct tape for the big bandages I was wearing so instead of going out to get more, Daddy used duct tape to hold them down. You were so pissed when you saw that, but you still stayed. You tried as best you could to remove the duct tape and bandages so that you could properly clean the wound. I don't remember being upset with you at the time, but I was very scared. I lived in constant fear that Daddy would try to kill me.

It would be two years before you tried to leave. When he convinced you to come back, I stood my ground and refused to go with either one of you. It was the first time I stood up for myself. I was nine. I shouldn't have had to choose myself and what was best for my well-being.

During that year, I didn't live with you and Daddy. When I finally went back to you two, I realized nothing had changed. Daddy was still drinking a lot, and by then, I was past angry. I didn't understand why you were still with him. But finally, a few months after, you left him for the final time. What should have been a celebration for us evolved into another situation that only angered me further. When you left my father, it was like you left my brother and me too. We barely saw you, and when we did, it was always with a different man.

The man who would later become my stepfather was weird. I did not like him, though I wasn't sure why. At the time, I was never able to put it into words. I just knew that I did not like that he used to walk into the room that I shared with my brother whenever he wanted. I locked the bedroom door at night because I had this fear that he would come in while we were sleeping.

One day, you went to work and did not come home for days. Our daddy came to pick us up. He told my brother and me that you had been arrested, and because of this, we would be living with him and our new stepmother. I was distraught. How could you leave us? And with the daddy I hated, of all people. Although I was glad that he no longer drank, he was still mean, and I did not want to be there. I felt as though I only existed in his house. I was not seen or heard, and I was constantly being compared to my stepsister. I was made to believe that I could not outshine her. When I began to act out of my character, Daddy bluntly told my brother and me that his only wish was that he'd given up his parental rights to the state. Sometimes he would even say to me, "You're going to grow up to be just like your mother." I hated you and I hated myself.

There were times I felt so alone. When I grew older, I moved back in with you and my stepfather. It was okay for a while, but my stepfather was still weird. His behaviors, like coming into my room unannounced, rubbing my leg when the two of us were driving somewhere, over-complimenting how good I looked or smelled, and slapping me across my behind one time when I was walking by him, all made me very uncomfortable. I was so scared to tell you, and honestly, I worried if you would even believe me. And just like I suspected, when I finally did tell you, you did not believe me. We got into a huge argument and fifteen years went by before we would actually speak again.

I've gone through so much and you were not there, including the birth of my two children and the grief of two failed marriages. We talk now from time to time but I'm still trying to get to a place where I can trust you and tell you how I feel. I fear you're not ready to hear my feelings and I also fear that telling you my truth will cause the little relationship you have with your husband to dissipate. None of what I am saying is to make you feel bad, but I need you to know that I've been hurt on so many levels and I just wished that you were there to protect me and love me through all of the bad times.

It's also heartbreaking that you missed out on all of the good times. Despite what I've been through, I'm still here, but I still can't help but think about the past. So this letter to you is my way of addressing the hurt. While I see both you and Daddy as human beings who are each on your own respective journeys, it took a long time for me to forgive you two for how I was treated. I'll always be reminded of you choosing my dad or my stepfather over me. That fact alone makes it hard for me to rebuild a relationship with you, and at times, my guard goes up. With time, I hope you have realized how these events have shaped and affected me. I ask that you be patient with me and more understanding of the fact that this relationship will take time to rebuild. In the meantime, please know that I love you.

Your Daughter

"Since the Lord is directing our steps, why try to understand everything that happens along the way?" Proverbs 20:24 (TLB)

Reflections

Use this space to write a memory, letter, or personal reflection.

"She is clothed with strength and dignity; she can laugh at the days to come. She speaks with wisdom, and faithful instruction is on her tongue." Proverbs 31:25-26 (NIV)

I Wasn't Ready

Reflecting on her own upbringing, a mother acknowledges how the absence of motherly nurturing shaped the way she mothered, while expressing deep regret for emotional gaps she now sees more clearly in the relationship with her own daughter. Interwoven in these reflections are tender memories of motherhood and grandmotherhood that reveal enduring love and connection. Ultimately, the letter is an honest plea for forgiveness, healing, and the possibility of rebuilding the mother–daughter bond with greater awareness and intention.

Dear Daughter,

I just realized something: my mother didn't really love me like she should. She didn't send me out into the world equipped with everything I should have known. I have a sharp tongue like hers, and while she tried to protect me, she partied almost every night until the time I left for the Navy. I was sad when I left, but I did not hate her. I could see the direction my life was taking, and I felt sorry for the life my mother had lived for so many years. Though she never physically abused me, the emotional scars were very prevalent. Nevertheless, I know she loved me the only way she knew how. Now it feels too late for both of us, especially since she has dementia. But this also tells me that it's not too late for us. We're both young at heart, and we both love my baby girl.

I tried so hard not to love or live like my mother did. I didn't have any baby nicknames or experience in how to raise a child, but I do know that I've loved you dearly. You had everything you needed and wanted for nothing—except candy. I said no to that because I didn't want your teeth to rot like mine did, and that was because I loved you. You had a bassinet, but you slept on my stomach for almost two years. You've always stayed clean and cute at every age. Back then, I thought I was ready for a baby, but after talking to you yesterday, I now realize I was selfish and didn't know it because I didn't have anyone to guide me through motherhood. I didn't love you the way I should have because I was young and lost in the streets, just like my mom. Despite my partying ways, I never left you with anyone who would ever hurt you; all the friends I trusted with you were very overprotective.

Truthfully, I didn't see the world then the way I do now. I closed myself off because I was free from the prison I lived in at home, and I didn't recognize the evil in people like I do now. You're not crazy, my baby; I'm the one who's crazy for not getting to know my daughter. I loved you the only way I knew how, which was a tough way. I never physically abused you and I would never do anything to harm my grandbaby either. I find child abuse very sick and sadistic and whoever abuses children should just die slowly. When you were growing up, I didn't let you go too much because I wished I had my mother around to guide me, instead of letting me go and then talking badly about me years later to you. I would never do that to your daughter, nor could I, because you're there with her every night.

Despite my small gestures to prove I was a worthy mom, I realize the harm my absence caused. I was in the streets until you left for the Navy, then I slowed down and eventually stopped being in the streets for years. My grandbaby came along, and I kept my little sunshine for you. I remember chasing her down the hall, catching her quick hands, pulling her out of the dog's food, and closing the bathroom, bedroom, and patio doors! I would turn my room into an obstacle course to keep her away from my jewelry. Sometimes, we would act like wrestlers and stomp around while she giggled. I would tickle her, and even though I was running out of breath from working a full day, this was something we did every day. It became our routine. I would never say anything bad about those moments. I loved them, and I miss them. I love you and I miss you. I would love nothing more than for you and my baby to come home.

Everyone has flaws, including me, so please forgive me for not giving you the love you deserve. I'm not a slow learner, but I now know how to love my daughter. Your screaming at me yesterday opened my ears, my eyes, and my heart. I promise you that. I'm ready to change and to be the mother you need and deserve.

I'm ready to love you the right way if you will have me. Please take all the time you need, but know I am here when you want me back as your mom. And if you don't forgive me, I will still always love you. You have always made me proud. I probably should've told you that sooner. I often wonder if that would have made a difference.

Love,

Mom

"Forgiveness is not an act of weakness; rather, it is a powerful testament to the resilience of the spirit and the depth of one's character."

Reflections

Use this space to write a memory, letter, or personal reflection.

"Her children rise up and call her blessed; her husband also, and he praises her: 'Many women have done excellently, but you surpass them all.'" Proverbs 31:28–29

Raising Queens:
A Mother's Love Letters to Her Daughters

A mother's love is displayed through journaling. She shares with us the joy her daughters bring to her life each day. In this letter, she's reminding them how the world can be challenging, yet it can also be rewarding. During difficult times, she encourages her daughters to always keep God at the forefront. And to always take care of one another. You shall be your sister's keeper.

Hello, my beautiful babies. The two of you are my greatest accomplishments. I don't know what my life would be like without you two. For the longest time, it has been the three of us, but there will be a time when I'm no longer around. I want to make sure that the two of you know how to take care of each other, but I also need you two to know how to survive on your own in this world because it can be cruel. While there are good people in it, there are also people who will see your light and try to dim it. These same people will go out of their way to break you down and steal your joy. I want you both to remember that regardless of what you will go through, God is always constant. I am raising you both to be women of God and my prayer is that you don't depart from that.

I will be honest and tell you that I wasn't always a woman of God. I experienced a lot of pain growing up that has affected my ability to love the two of you the way you both need to be loved. Thankfully, I became aware of where I was going wrong and each day I strive to be the best mother that I can be to both of you. I am writing this letter to you both as tangible reassurance of my love for you.

To my oldest,

I was so young when I had you. I was basically a child myself and didn't know what I was doing, but I knew that when I saw your face for the first time, I fell in love with you. I admire how independent you have always been, but I feel that I failed you in your earlier years because I put pressure on you to be self-sufficient. I now realize that I should have been checking in with you in order to understand your mental and spiritual health. There were times when I was too hard on you, and for that, I am so sorry.

You have told me that you thought I hated you and that broke me. Yes, you have done things that have disappointed me, but it is my job to help you pivot your behavior. I could never hate you. As you've grown older, boys have started taking an interest in you. Always remember that your body is a temple. Never feel pressured to do something that you do not want to do. Respect and love yourself and release anyone who cannot respect your boundaries. Anyone who is meant to be in your life will be in your life. Be safe in everything that you do. Anytime you are filled with conviction, that is a sign that what you are doing is wrong. Seek God ALWAYS! I am guilty of running from God, and I am here to tell you that my life was so hard because I made it harder than it needed to be. I thought I knew everything when I didn't know anything. Remember to have humility. You will make mistakes and there is nothing wrong with saying you're sorry and asking for forgiveness. Explore the world and do what moves you. Don't let anyone put limits on you. If you want to pursue art, then do just that. I will support you in whatever you decide to do. I know that you will do great things. You have always been wise beyond your years, and I can't wait to see the woman that you will become. I love you and I thank you for your patience as we take strides to rebuild our relationship.

To my Baby Girl,

You have always kept me on my toes since the day you took your first breath! To learn that your personality is who I was at your age is a breath of fresh air. You're so smart and inquisitive and just full of life. Having you has made me be more intentional about how I want to continue to raise you and your sister. Every day you teach me patience. When I look at your little face, I see nothing but pure love. While you are too young to understand certain things that happen around you, you do understand who God is, and I love how you want to get to know Him.

There are a few things that I need you to know. The first is that I love you. You've asked about your father and why he and I are not together. While I can't tell you everything until you are older, I will say that we are not together because things didn't work out between us. Even though things didn't work out, it doesn't mean that he and I don't love you, and trust me when I say that it had nothing to do with you. I'm sorry that your father is not in your life the way that you want and need him to be. I'm praying that he does better in life for your sake so that you can grow with a father who you can admire and respect. In the meantime, you have your sister and me and just know that we got you. I will protect you both with everything that I have in me. Enjoy being a child and growing up. I see that you also like art and while you make messes with your glitter and other supplies, I am proud to see the perspective that you have on life and how carefree you are. Anytime I am having a bad day, you do something silly to make me laugh. You have no idea how much I need and appreciate that. You can't stand seeing me upset, and at times, I've felt ashamed that you had to see that vulnerable side of me. Continue being you and sharing your joy with others. I will also tell you to love and respect yourself and your body. Also, live your life without limits. Always keep God first and know that He is there whenever you need Him.

The final thing that I want to make sure the two of you understand is that the three of us are FAMILY. I know that we don't look traditional. We have each other and the two of you have each other. Take care of each other, protect one another, and love each other. I'm so proud of both of you. I know Mama can be strict at times, but know my love for the two of you is unwavering and everything I do is so you two don't grow up to make the same mistakes that I did.

I love you so much and always.

-Mama

"I will instruct you and teach you in the way you should go; I will counsel you with my eye upon you." Psalm 32:8 (NIV)

Reflections

Use this space to write a memory, letter, or personal reflection.

"Teach me, O Lord, the way of your statutes, and I shall keep it to the end. Give me understanding, and I shall keep your law indeed, I shall observe it with my whole heart." Psalm 119:33 (NLT)

Deep Seated Dependency

While dependency can create a sense of connection and support, it can also lead to unforeseen challenges when that balance is disrupted. A daughter shares a letter reflecting on the emotions surrounding her mother's death, a moment that profoundly shifted her perspective on life. The letter further explores her realization that independence can sometimes feel like a double-edged sword, offering both strength and loneliness.

Dear Mommy,

First, I want to thank you for loving me and being the best mom. You protected me, but most importantly, you loved me abundantly and unconditionally. You were my best friend and the best mother a child could pray for.

Though we had our differences, we also shared many likes, like shopping. I can't really blame you for our closeness, but I'm sad and angry about feeling like you crippled my growth, and then you left me to fend on my own. You showed me how to always depend on you, but not how to rely on myself. All in all, I still learned so many valuable lessons that helped me grow into a strong woman. You taught me to know my worth and to love myself and others. I remember the prayer you would say with me as a child: "Now I lay me down to sleep, I pray to the Lord my soul to keep. If I shall die before I wake, I pray to the Lord my soul to take. God bless me, God bless Mommy and Daddy, and God bless my family." That was our prayer and I loved it. I still love it —so much so that I start my nightly prayers off with that same prayer to this day. I know Mommy...but that is my way of praying with you.

But Mommy, I'm angry with you for leaving me! I prayed every day and night that you would fight to stay with me. I needed you. What would happen to me if you left? No one understood me like you did. After you left, all I saw was darkness. Why would God take you away from me? I needed and wanted you back. So, I worked around the clock and barely slept to try not to think about you. I rarely ate; my sugar levels were all out of whack. Anger and sadness consumed me. I suffered multiple strokes and felt helpless. All I wanted was to be with you. But Dad, your husband, was there to pick up the pieces. More importantly, he not only helped me heal, he forced me into self-sufficiency by making me move out of the family home. Dad told me the one thing I needed to hear: "You have to live and take care of yourself, but I'll be there for you whenever you need me." He said I had to try for myself first, and if I fell, he would be there to help me back up. And you know what? He was—and he still is. Even though doctors and others have labeled me as handicapped, I don't consider myself handicapped. I am doing better living on my own. There are some things I still cannot do for myself, but Dad comes over to help me maintain the upkeep of the house. I am thinking about leaving home altogether. There are too many memories for me here. Dad is the only one I have contact with. You already know who rarely speaks and she has moved away already.

I'm no longer angry with you for leaving me. I've learned to feel your presence and your grace. I know that you are always with me. I feel you emotionally and physically, especially in the moments when it's time to start my day. You let me know you're with me by gently tapping my left foot, encouraging me to get out of bed. I now understand that you left me to be with me, so I could grow into the woman you knew I could be. You never knew that I was afraid to be alone. I never knew until you died, because you were always right there with me. I do not know how to be without you, but I promise to trust God and learn to live. I love you, Mommy, always.

-Your Girl

"I will lead the blind on unfamiliar roads. I will lead them on unfamiliar paths. I will turn darkness into light in front of them." Isaiah 42:16 (GOD'S WORD Translation)

Reflections

Use this space to write a memory, letter, or personal reflection.

"Fret not yourself because of evildoers; be not envious of wrongdoers! For they will soon fade like the grass and wither like the green herb. Trust in the Lord and do good; dwell in the land and befriend faithfulness. Delight yourself in the Lord, and he will give you the desires of your heart. Commit your way to the Lord; trust in him, and he will act." Psalm 37:1

I Get It from My Mama

We all sometimes daydream of those epic mommy-daughter moments — whether they are memories we've cherished, experiences we've already shared, or new trips we look forward to planning. This letter details appreciation and gratitude for all of them. A daughter wants her Mama to know that everything fabulous about her comes from her mother.

Dear Ma,

I just wanted to take a moment to tell you how much I appreciate you. Words will never fully capture the gratitude I have for everything you have done for me, but I want you to know that I see it, I feel it, and I carry it with me every day.

Your guidance, wisdom, and unwavering support have shaped me into the woman I am today. You have been my teacher, role model, and biggest cheerleader. Through your generosity—whether it was your time, your love, or your sacrifices—you have shown me what it truly means to be strong, kind, and selfless.

You have also taught me how to be firm, assertive, and to stand my ground. Because of you, I know how to navigate life's challenges with confidence and grace. You showed me that strength is not just about resilience, but also about knowing my worth, speaking up for myself, and never backing down from what I believe in.

Every lesson you've taught me, every moment you've stood by my side, has made an impact that I will carry with me forever. Thank you for being you. Thank you for loving me the way you do. I am so blessed to have you as my mom, and I will always be grateful to you.

Love,

Your Daughter

"Strife and dignity she can laugh at the days to come, she speaks with wisdom, and faithful instruction is on her tongue." Proverbs 31:25-26

Reflections

Use this space to write a memory, letter, or personal reflection.

"Never avenge yourself, but leave the way open for God's wrath."
Romans 12:19 (AMP)

Same Daughter, Newer Truth

In the face of disagreement, unconditional love should remain steadfast. A mother shares her journey of raising a teenage daughter amid her own personal trauma. Acknowledging the stressors that created distance between them, she hopes that by embracing openness and trust, they can nurture a bond rooted in security and empathy.

Dear Daughter,

I see you and the new challenges you're beginning to face. Always remember that life is not always fair, and how we handle its lessons determines our outcome. Life itself can be overwhelming as you navigate your teenage years. I can only imagine how difficult it must be; nevertheless, if you continue to share with me, I promise to acknowledge your feelings. When you feel uncertain and/or frustrated, I'll be here for you. I am here for all of it because those are your feelings, and they are valid.

When you came to me about your struggles with your sexuality, I heard you. Allowing yourself to be who you are is a brave step. Although it was difficult for me to hear as your mother, I admire your strength and courage in having that conversation with me. Understanding how difficult the conversation about you being gay would be, you did it anyway, which reassures me that your resilience will guide you through life, even when I am not here.

If I'm being honest, there are a few issues I'm struggling with. While I fully support you as my daughter, I'm still having a hard time understanding the decision you've made to live your life as a gay teenager, and very soon, as a young woman. The way your style of dress changed to masculine so drastically, overnight, caught me by surprise. You expected me to be comfortable with that and to just adapt, but it wasn't that easy for me.

Dating is a subject I've purposely shied away from with you. I've always told you 16 was your magic number for dating and your Junior prom is this year. This situation is definitely going to have to be revisited. It goes against everything I have taught you thus far, and what I still stand for. I do not support you dating another female. Approaching this topic feels like the start of a rift between us. I don't want to claim that, and the thought of it hurts my soul! I feel like I'm going to lose you once you leave for college. I struggle with this possibility EVERY DAY! I'm sitting here in tears as I think about it. I even feel like a hypocrite because I encourage you to come and talk to me, and I have been too afraid to chart these waters. This conversation can get deep. I have been keeping it inside. I don't know if I ever told you this, but BRO! I thought that I had this on lock (that's what you young kids say). I pray that you do not think of me as a coward because I've never shared this, but I don't! I don't have this on lock at all! But after much prayer, what I can tell you is that I have joined an LGBTQ parent support group to help me with some of my issues. I'm genuinely trying to learn and understand your perspective, challenges, and anything you may be going through. I love you Hepka.

While it may seem like I don't always understand what you are going through, I do genuinely want to grow with you. I pray that our relationship remains a safe space where you feel comfortable expressing yourself, discussing your thoughts, and sharing your dreams and fears. You don't have to hide anything from me—I am always here to listen, without judgment.

When the doctor told me I was having a little girl, I was instantly filled with fear about everything that I thought could happen to you, and how I would not be able to protect you. What I came to realize is that while I was financially prepared to become your momma, I was not mentally ready. I had been running away from healing for so long. I felt like no one understood the depths of what happens to a child when someone they love disappoints and hurts them. I lost my 13-year-old self after a traumatic experience when I was in the 8th grade. I was raped by my basketball coach. First, I felt like it was my fault because I laid there in fear. Then rage filled my body, and that is when I decided I was telling on his ass! I laid down a victim. However, when it was over, I ROSE a defender and a protector. And to think, he had the nerve to take me back to school as if nothing had happened. I reported him immediately. My mother asked me if it was the truth. What she did not realize at that time was that she was the first one to ever question my integrity. My own mom.

What she actually said: "ARE YOU TELLING THE TRUTH?"

What I heard: "YOU TELLING A LIE."

I never told my mom I held on to the fact that I called her for a ride that morning and she told me no because she had already woken me before she left for work. She had, but I just didn't get up. I am sharing this with you now because I held on to something for so long that it ate away at my relationship with my mother and now, my daughter. For fear that something might happen to you, I kept you from discovering your passion and love for basketball, or anything else that required you to have a "coach." I think you hate me for this at times, but I am not going to apologize for protecting you the way any mother would. But I do apologize that my protection may prohibit you from pursuing some of your desires. I might even admit that I could lighten up just a bit.

In 2019, you told me how angry you were with me. I didn't understand because of the sacrifices I have made for you, and that's how I responded, angrily. How about some gratitude? I will never forget how you looked at me and said, "Why did I have to be your sacrifice? I just wanted my mom." My heart ached for a long time. I wanted you to remember that for your eighth birthday, your only request was for me to quit the military, so I quit (retired). But I never knew mothers weren't allowed to hurt or have feelings. Whoever said that is a liar! My then nine-year-old had a lot to say to me, and because of our relationship, you knew it was safe to tell me during our kitchen table talk. I had to take it and bear it.

I want you to be reminded that I was once a teenager and I understand all too well how life can seem unfair when your mother doesn't give you free reign to do as you please. I thought my mom was being too hard on me at times, but one day I realized she's actually the smartest person I know. Her every decision for my life had a purpose. I knew that she wanted at least one of her children to follow in her footsteps, and because I was an average student, your grandmother made me go to college. I was the only one to graduate from high school, because I couldn't let my mother down, right? While I was in school, I learned early on, back in 1994, what FAAFO (F*** Around and Find Out) truly meant. My mother showed up at what was my first apartment off-campus with a U-Haul truck, along with your uncles and a few of their friends. I will never forget that day. We had just dropped some fried chicken, doing what college kids do. I had no idea she was coming, but I should have guessed after she received my grades for that semester. Moving back home after living on my own was not easy. I craved the military so I tried the Army first, thinking this recruiter would stand up to my mother. Nope, your grandmother cursed that recruiter out so badly with made-up words that your cousin was talking in tongues and trying to apologize to that man. Needless to say, I did not join the Army. All these rules had to go. However, I was 20 years old, living in her house. Her house, her rules.

While my mother was visiting Italy, the Marine recruiter took me for the ASVAB test. Let me tell you how God works. As I was sitting there, the Navy recruiter walked by. He looked at me as I looked back at him. He asked if I really wanted to enlist in the Marines. I said no, then shared my story with him. As a result, I took the Armed Services Vocational Aptitude Battery test and ultimately joined the Navy.

Twenty-four years later, that same Navy recruiter was the keynote speaker at my retirement ceremony. My mother was filled with gratitude for saving her daughter's life. He stated that I had repaid him by enlisting his son, who is now an officer, into the Navy. We have become family. Additionally, that recruiter became a counselor under your grandmother's guidance. While I may not have always liked her point of view, I know that she was always looking out for me – the same way I'm always looking out for you.

We might not always see eye to eye, but I hope you understand that my intentions come from a place of love and care. I want nothing but the best for you. I will always support you in your journey, even if my suggestions sometimes feel challenging. I am learning too, and we can find a way through together. Always remember, it's okay to feel what you are feeling. Change is complicated, but necessary. We face it together and with patience. I believe in you.

I love you to the moon and back!

Always,

Mom

"And let the peace (soul harmony which comes) from Christ rule (act as umpire continually) in your hearts [deciding and settling with finality all questions that arise in your minds, in that peaceful state] to which as [members of Christ's] one body you were also called [to live]. And be thankful (appreciative), [giving praise to God always]." Colossians 3:15 AMPC

Reflections

Use this space to write a memory, letter, or personal reflection.

____

____

____

____

____

____

____

____

____

____

____

____

____

____

____

____

____

"He said, 'If you listen carefully to the Lord your God and do what is right in his eyes, if you pay attention to his commands and keep all his decrees, I will not bring on you any of the diseases I brought on the Egyptians, for I am the Lord, who heals you.'" Exodus 15:26 (NLT)

Help Me Understand

Have you ever heard phrases like: "You are the strongest one; they needed me more than you did," or "I knew I wasn't going to have to worry about you?" This letter reflects on how a daughter has internalized such sentiments, believing that her brothers were favored during their upbringing. It explores how these feelings have shaped her relationship with her mother over the years. While the daughter expresses gratitude for her mother's unwavering support, there are also hints of hurt and a sense of loss. This reflection reveals the dynamics of family life, where love and pain often intertwine, encouraging readers to connect with the writer's experiences and the complicated nature of maternal relationships.

To My Mother:

I have spent a great deal of my life telling anyone who would listen that my mother and I have the best relationship. I want to thank you for never giving up on me. I've always told you I wanted to be just like you, but your response was, "No ma'am, you be better than me." The love and support that you showed me was always unwavering and unmatched. I love you more today than ever before. Thank God that I was part of your assignment.

Against your wishes, I enlisted in the military at 21. Responding to the recruiter when he asked me why, "My mother has three children, and if anything were to happen to her, I need to be capable of providing care for her." I was 21 years old when I said that and I still mean it today! I am ready to be the woman you raised me to be.

When I left home, you were still in your early 50s, full of life. Now that I have returned and have a family of my own, I encounter a different person altogether. No one is trying to meet the new you. I realize this transformation must have started while I was away working, but it feels abrupt and disheartening to me. I am afraid of what I see every time I come home. I've never been anxious about change; however, seeing you change right before my eyes has made me HATE THE AIR I BREATHE.

Every time I attempt to voice my concerns about you to my siblings, the disdain is clearly felt. Strangely enough, it's those very siblings whom I always believed you favored, the ones who received most of your attention. But now, as an adult, I understand their treatment was never about being favored—it was simply a matter of differences in your three children. People often say they can forgive but can't forget, and I find myself caught in that struggle.

I try to forget the day you chose not to press charges against my brother for stealing thousands of dollars from your account. Perhaps I could have moved past that incident, but it weighed heavily on my heart for another reason. You were recently wrongfully terminated and had no income to fall back on, while I had just received a settlement. Your words stung as they fell out of your mouth: "I don't want to be the reason my son spends time in jail."

Yet, my brother, your son, took advantage of that vulnerable moment, knowing full hell well that you were struggling. In that instant, I felt the heartbreaking reality: you were faced with a choice, and you chose him. You always did. I have a question: Why does it seem natural to coddle sons while raising daughters to take on more responsibility? Studies have shown that mothers tend to be more critical of their daughters and more permissive toward their sons. I don't need written proof; I experienced it firsthand throughout my adulthood. People often said I was mature for my age, but I felt like you interpreted that as meaning I didn't need you as much. My brothers' poor choices were already causing you sleepless nights. I heard you crying so many times over something one of them did or didn't do. I wanted to hug you every time, but you always said you were fine. You weren't, were you?

You and I were in a conversation that made me think back to when my last name was different. It prompted me to search for someone. That someone was a man who turned out to be my biological father. It was the same man who you previously told me was not my father. I asked you at age seven and again at 30 years old. What hurt me this time was that I gave you an opportunity to talk to me when I became an adult, but you still refused to tell me the truth. I know that raising children does not come with instructions. The only book I know of is the Bible and you taught me that the Bible teaches us to forgive.

Everything God does has a reason, and the same goes for what a mother does. I tried to connect with my father, and through that, I realized why it was best to keep his identity from me. I learned that he hit you when he was jealous. He also shared with me why he spent time in prison. It all came back to me! You would punish my brothers for teasing me about MY daddy being in jail for decapitating a man after a robbery. That further confused me, because all I ever knew was that we all had the same father. I met a younger brother and sister. Neither of them were too excited to learn they had a sister, and that I was his first child. In short, they did not want to pursue a relationship with me. And yes, my biological father included. I was able to connect with one of his sisters, however. It felt good to hear she wanted to get to know me. Unknowing if you would support that relationship, I've kept it from you, not wanting to cause any further hurt after speaking with my father.

I understand that you made decisions for our well-being, and never again will I question any of them. I won't open any topics you've chosen to leave closed concerning my father and I apologize if my questions triggered anything when I turned 30. Since then, I've been working on my mental health, and I realized I might have triggered some memories you would rather forget. It was never my intention to do so and I'm sorry for that. I love you Mother, and I know you did your best for us. I am forever grateful. I have grown from accepting my past; I am a better person for it. The life lessons you taught equipped me to handle what this world has for me. Although we may face new challenges, if we commit to open dialogue and honesty without any judgment or blame, We Win!

–DAUGHTER

"May He grant you out of the riches of His glory, to be strengthened and spiritually energized with power through His Spirit in your inner self, [indwelling your innermost being and personality], so that Christ may dwell in your hearts through your faith." Ephesians 3:16-17

Reflections

Use this space to write a memory, letter, or personal reflection.

"Is anyone among you sick? Let them call the elders of the church to pray over them and anoint them with oil in the name of the Lord. And the prayer offered in faith will make the sick person well; the Lord will raise them up. If they have sinned, they will be forgiven." James 5:14-15

Free From Blame

A daughter reflects on a childhood marked by emotional absence and limited joyful memories, while writing from a place of maturity rather than anger. Grounded in her faith, she offers compassion and forgiveness, recognizing the trauma her mother endured and how it shaped their relationship. The letter ultimately extends an invitation to healing, grace, and the possibility of rebuilding their bond through understanding and shared growth.

Dear Mama,

It's taken me 43 years to say this, but the time has come for me to write to you without anger. And while I want to also say without pain, I can't quite confirm yet, as I am fighting back the tears.

As I think back over my childhood, I try to remember our happy moments, and the truth is, they are few and far between. I am not saying this, or anything else in this letter, to hurt you, but rather help you understand me and our relationship now. My hope is that after reading it, we can progress towards healing. I will say this again: my hope and intention in writing this letter is for you to get a better understanding of me and our relationship in the past, and then to heal, and move forward in a more loving, healthy relationship.

I do not blame you for all the awful things that happened to me as a child. At 43, my relationship with God has helped me to understand that everything that happened to me was already written and had to happen for me to become the woman I am today. I did not always feel this way, but that is what God, growth, maturity, grace, and mercy will do. You were a teenage mother, a high school dropout, physically abused, and later battled with an addiction to crack cocaine. You may not remember, but I remember so much about your story that even now as I think about it, I truly understand where I get my strength and resilience.

Sadly, much of your strength and resilience evolved from dark circumstances, from being molested by my father and other family members at nine, to being placed in foster care at 10, and getting pregnant at 12. Recognizing your journey, I cannot blame you for not being there when I needed you. You know what else? I forgive you and release you from the guilt and shame that any of that brings to you, if any. You were fighting your own battles. You were not given the love, attention, and nurturing as a child that you were owed, so how could you give it to me?

In closing, I want you to know that you and I had to endure those horrible things to be who we are today. God trusted us just as He trusted Job, and look at us now. I thought that there was a possibility I would feel pain while writing this letter, but nope! I also started, then stopped, went to sleep, and woke up fresh with the presence of God as I finished it. There is so much I want to say, so I decided to do it in layers. This is the beginning of many letters, as I want you to really heal and process it all layer by layer. That takes time, as it took me years. It is a beautiful journey, and I hope that you'll take it with me. I love you and I am proud to be your daughter, your firstborn child, the one who started you on your journey of motherhood to be who you are today.

Always,

Your Baby Girl

"The LORD also will be a refuge for the oppressed, a refuge in times of trouble." Psalm 9:9

Reflections

Use this space to write a memory, letter, or personal reflection.

"She is clothed with strength and dignity; she can laugh at the days to come." Proverbs 31:25

The Mother Who Chose Me

Showing deep gratitude to her adoptive mother and acknowledging the challenges of their past, a daughter reflects on her mother's choice to support her and her siblings despite the difficulties they faced together. She shares painful childhood experiences, including trauma and fears, as well as regrets about lost time during her mother's illness. Ultimately, she recognizes the valuable lessons learned about love, selflessness, and accountability.

Hey Mom,

There's so much on my mind I want to share with you. It's hard to determine where to begin, but here it goes.

Thank you for being the incredible person you are—truly a gift from God. I've often wondered about your decision to step in as our mom when my biological parents were unable to care for my siblings and me. What motivated you to embrace that role? Your commitment to us filled a void I didn't even fully understand at the time, and for that, I am grateful to you. Thank you for being a steady force in my upbringing and for helping me to become the woman I am today. Yet, I must confess that there were dark moments in my childhood that I never shared with you. When I was just five, I experienced things that no little girl should have to endure involving your adult son. I kept those painful memories locked away, fearing you wouldn't believe me or that it would break your heart. I worried about being taken away and separated from my brothers, so I chose silence instead. As time passed and I grew older, I eventually found the courage to tell my husband and my brothers about what happened to me. I am grateful that these experiences didn't haunt me or drive me to despair. Through it all, I now see that God was guarding my mind and heart.

The loss of my foster dad sent me into a whirlwind of emotions. At age 16, I didn't fully grasp the depths of your grief during that time, but I felt a strange sense of freedom without the rigid structure that had kept me in check. It's only now, as an adult, that I understand the love and concern behind his strictness.

In navigating my rebellious phase, I faced consequences I wasn't prepared for. I became a teenage mother at just 18, and it was a stark wake-up call. I still struggle with the memory of your daughter kicking me out, which felt like a betrayal. That moment forced me to mature quickly and find my own strength, pushing me to become a responsible wife to my now husband, who has loved me since the eighth grade.

For a long time, I failed to see how my decisions led to our estrangement. When we finally reconnected, it was heartbreaking to witness the effects of dementia robbing you of life's vibrant moments. My children never had the chance to know the wonderful woman you were, and I deeply regret that you missed out on so many precious moments in our lives together.

As I write this today, I can't help but reflect on the fact that it is the anniversary of your funeral—three years since you left this world to return to God.   My heart aches with the weight of missed opportunities and conversations that should have happened. I wish I had been more present in your life, cherishing the moments when we could have built a stronger bond. But even in the pain of lost time, I find comfort in knowing that God recognizes the love you poured into my life.

You have taught me what it truly means to love—to be selfless, to give without expecting anything in return, and to keep faith at the forefront of my life. Thank you for having the courage to make tough decisions and for guiding me to take responsibility for my poor choices. Your unwavering strength as a black mother has left an undeniable mark on my heart, shaping me into who I am today.

I love you more than words can express, and I carry your lessons with me every day. Job well done, Mom. Your legacy will live on in me, and I promise to honor it in all I do.

I'll Always Love You,

Forever your daughter

"Be strong and courageous. Do not be afraid or terrified because of them, for the LORD your God goes with you; He will never leave you nor forsake you." Deuteronomy 31:6

Reflections

Use this space to write a memory, letter, or personal reflection.

____

____

____

____

____

____

____

____

____

____

____

____

____

____

____

____

____

____

"The LORD is close to the brokenhearted and saves those who are crushed in spirit." Psalm 34:18 (NLT)

#MOM.COM

A teenage daughter reflects on an honest conversation with her mother regarding her newfound sexuality. Feeling the heavy burden of her mother's discomfort, tension starts to invade their once-close bond. She is very thankful for her mother's support and care throughout her life and yearns to preserve their connection. Though this conversation sparks thunder in their relationship, she prays their history of love can still weather any storm.

Today, my mom and I had a long and difficult conversation about my sexuality. This particular topic of conversation has become an emotional subject for both of us. I sense her discomfort whenever anything comes up about the subject of being gay. Knowing her and how she is raising me weighs heavily on my heart. I know she does not approve. During our discussion, she revealed her feelings of how my being gay has dramatically damaged our relationship. Her words left me feeling confused, hurt and angry. Not to mention, questioning how my attraction to the same sex could carry such profound implications that alter the dynamics of our entire relationship. This is overwhelming.

What I really believe my mother wanted to say was that my sexuality changed the way she thinks of me. It's hard to grasp how something so personal to me could make her so upset that she nearly sheds a tear whenever it's discussed. Simply mentioning who I am and the fact that

I am comfortable with myself often leads to uncomfortable conversations. She even went so far as to compare my being gay to losing me to society and becoming depressed, as if my identity means I can't be what she wants me to be. I've tried to explain that this has nothing to do with society, but I believe she just isn't ready to accept having a gay daughter. It scares me that she thinks our entire relationship has changed because of who I am attracted to.

My mom frequently asks if I'm happy at home. I used to feel content and at ease, but lately, my sense of happiness has been diminishing. I've come to realize that while she offers her support in many ways, she struggles to fully accept me and my identity, as well as the community I belong to. This lack of acceptance adds to my feeling of isolation. Sometimes I find myself questioning whether it would have been better for me to stay in the closet, where I felt less pressure to confront her discomfort and potentially avoid the problems in our relationship.

From an early age, I've always known that my mom is my greatest supporter. She has fought tirelessly for me, standing up for my dreams and aspirations. Her fierce advocacy has been a constant presence in my life since I took my first breath. I love her for that every single day. Of course, like any other mother and daughter, we've had our share of ups and downs. There have been moments of frustration and heated disagreements, but through it all, I've come to understand that her love for me remains committed and unchanging. No matter the circumstances, she has always been my strongest supporter.

My mom is not just the most important woman in my life; she is the most important person in my life. She is my rock during my most challenging times, and the one who believed in me when I struggled to believe in myself. I can still recall many nights when she stayed up late helping me with homework or comforting me after a tough day at school. I know that I do not express to her how grateful I am for all that she has done for me. I am going to change that and try to show her every chance I get. Truthfully, there are times when I feel unworthy of her efforts and love, but I'm constantly trying to think of creative ways to show her just how much I love her.

Mom, I want you to know how much you mean to me. I truly cherish our relationship and hope it stays as close as it has always been. You're such an incredible person, and I'm deeply grateful for everything you do. I love you with all my heart. I promise to always mean it, just as you have taught me. Thank you for being such an incredible momma!

With love,

Your daughter

"Cast your burden on the Lord [releasing the weight of it], and He will sustain you; He will never allow the [consistently] righteous to be moved (made to slip, fall, or fail)." Psalms 55:22

Reflections

Use this space to write a memory, letter, or personal reflection.

____

____

____

____

____

____

____

____

____

____

____

____

____

____

____

____

____

____

"Come to Me, all you who labor and are heavy laden, and I will give you rest. Take My yoke upon you and learn from Me, for I am gentle and lowly in heart, and you will find rest for your souls. For My yoke is easy and My burden is light." Matthew 11:28-30

Military Brat

A retired veteran and single mother grapples with the challenges of her relationship with her daughter, especially since leaving the military. As her daughter matures, the mother is constantly reminded of the time they missed together during her service. While she found it easy to show up for her Jr. sailors, she is struggling to do the same for her daughter. The battles she faced in combat seem trivial compared to the emotional struggle of reconnecting with her daughter, who is now discovering her own voice and identity. Even during her many deployments, the mother fought to return home to her daughter, making the adjustment to civilian life and motherhood even more difficult.

Dear Daughter,

As I take a moment to reflect on my life and the journey we've shared thus far, I find myself wishing I had approached many situations differently, so I could truly convey to you just how much you mean to me. I realize one of the first steps I need to take in strengthening our relationship is forgiving myself for the circumstances from which you were conceived. Your father, being a married man, then choosing to be an absentee father was never part of the future I imagined for myself, and certainly not for us as a family. That unexpected reality had a profoundly negative impact on our lives for so long, and in ways I never would have anticipated. I pray that you are able to forgive me for the years I could not be the mother that you so rightly deserved, only because I could not see the blessing over my pain.

From the very beginning, my focus has always been on supporting, guiding, and protecting you. However, I sometimes worry that in my desire to make up for the time we lost, I may unintentionally push you further away. It hurts to see you shouldering so much on your own, and there are moments when I feel powerless to offer the help you need.

Believe it or not, there are times when I wonder if you're ever proud of me, just as I feel an overwhelming sense of pride for you. Watching you grow into your own person—making decisions, facing challenges, and becoming a young woman—fills me with joy. I often see pieces of myself in your kindness and strength, and I need you to know that your potential is truly limitless. You possess incredible fortitude; I encourage you to tap into that inner strength as you navigate life's ups and downs.

Admittedly, I sometimes worry that your caring nature—your ability to connect with anyone and everyone—might cloud your judgment when it comes to choosing friends. I recall how challenging it was for you to form any type of lasting bond during our numerous moves, and I've always wanted you to know that following your heart is essential. Remember, investments are not just about money; they also include your time, emotions, and energy. What you choose to nurture will flourish, much like a beautifully tended lawn.

I know that my work absences during those long months, sometimes lasting an entire year, must have filled you with confusion and, at times, anger. It must have shattered your spirits to have to question the sacrifices I made, and ultimately to wonder if you were the sacrifice. Let me assure you, I never wanted you to feel that way. My prayer is that someday you will understand the love that fueled the many hard choices I had to make daily. Every decision I made was rooted in my love for you. I will not apologize for my life before you; it shaped both of us into who we are today. I have worked very hard to equip you with the knowledge and resources needed to thrive, ensuring that if I were to leave this world tomorrow, you would stand strong as the remarkable woman I know you will become. My love for you has remained steadfast, even during times that we disagreed, argued, and even when I had to discipline you. Nothing could ever change the bond we share.

There have been many times when I've wanted to simply embrace you wholeheartedly and apologize for not fully considering your perspective while I fought with my own. I now realize how important it is for both of us to learn and grow together. I am committed to fostering an open dialogue between us where we can share our experiences and support each other in our individual journeys. Moving forward, I hope we can strengthen our connection by understanding and appreciating our differences, and the challenges we've each faced.

I truly appreciate your patience as I navigated my own challenges in adulthood, many of which stemmed from my upbringing. Considering that, I have identified a few personal issues I believe may have impacted our relationship that I would like to share with you. You always said I sometimes smothered you, a pattern influenced by my own childhood experiences. Unfortunately, I was not given a space to express myself freely. My tendency to say "no" came far too easily, often without considering your feelings or needs. I understand that this might have affected your confidence and sense of independence, and for that, I sincerely apologize. I talked *at* you, as opposed to having a real, honest conversation *with* you. It may sometimes feel like it's too late to make amends, but I want you to know that I'm aware of my shortcomings and am committed to changing.

Through therapy and our shared commitment to personal growth, it is apparent that our relationship has evolved in meaningful ways. We've built a foundation of trust and open communication. I pray we continue on this path. You may not remember this because you were so young, but my fondest memories are the moments we spent crafting, picking strawberries together, learning to ride horses, or just exploring the park and museums, where our laughter filled the air. I also treasure our cozy Friday movie nights, curled up on the couch with blankets and popcorn, where we had a real connection in the simple act of just being together. These experiences remind me of the dreams I used to have before you were born or even conceived. Though we have faced numerous challenges, I remain in place. There were times when it felt like it was just the two of us against the world, and I cherish the strength of that bond. Our mantra has always been: ME: TEAMWORK/YOU: MAKES THE DREAM WORK!

Love,

Mom

"But you all must be strong and not lose heart, for there is a reward for your deeds." 2 Chronicles 15:7 (NIV)

Reflections

Use this space to write a memory, letter, or personal reflection.

"She speaks with wisdom, and faithful instruction is on her tongue." Proverbs 31:26

Simply the Best

In "Simply the Best," a daughter expresses deep appreciation for the loving, supportive relationship she shares with her mother. She reflects on how her mother's patience, encouragement, and respect helped shape her confidence and independence from childhood into adulthood. Acknowledging her mother's own upbringing, she recognizes the many ways love was shown through actions rather than words. The letter ultimately celebrates the natural evolution of their bond into a genuine friendship rooted in mutual respect, trust, and enduring love.

Hey Mom,

I have never told you this, but you are my best friend. You have always made it easy for me to share my thoughts and I look forward to our talks every day. Your interest in everything I wanted to do gave me the strength and confidence to embrace new endeavors and you always told me that you were proud of me. You have been a patient mother. You've recognized when I was going through tough times and genuinely offered comfort and advice when I've asked for it.

I know my grandparents were not very affectionate toward you or your siblings, which is why hugging may seem unnatural to you. However, through every action in my life, you have shown that your love is here to stay. You never shared how sad you were when I left home; instead, you embraced my independence. I don't recall the transition from parent-child to friendship being difficult; it felt natural. You have also made a similar transition as a grandmother. You don't parent your grandkids; rather, you give them love and spoil my kids whenever you can.

Your perspective on raising me has always been, "You can't expect respect from your child if you don't respect them, too." You guided, taught, and disciplined me when necessary. Because you were more of a parent than a friend while I was growing up, I now understand our relationship dynamics much better. Thank you for allowing me to find my independence early, within reason, of course.

I've learned that the most challenging part of parenting is letting go, but that is what ultimately strengthens our bond. Thank you for simply being you, Mom. I love you so much.

Love,

Your Daughter

"For where your treasure is, there your heart will be also." Luke 12:34 (NKJV)

Reflections

Use this space to write a memory, letter, or personal reflection.

"Behold, I was brought forth in iniquity, and in sin my mother conceived me. Behold, you desire truth, the innermost being, and in the hidden part, you will make me know wisdom. Purify me with hyssop, and I shall be clean; Wash me, and I shall be whiter than snow." Psalms 51:5-7

Family Secrets

Why is it that I feel different? Could this be my imagination? As a child, I could not understand what was going on until that day when all my questions were answered. Yet, my world, as I knew it, was turned upside down, and now I finally understood —but not really! I invite you to examine my truth. A pivotal adult moment, marked by the revealing of my biological father in the most shattering way.

Dear Mama,

I wish I had known sooner, like as a child, why I felt like someone who did not belong in the family. I wondered why I was the only reader in the house, the only writer in the house, and the only one who talked back. I distinctly remember always escaping into the characters in whatever story I was reading to forget about the harshness of our life, or why I often felt like a child who was either favored too much or treated harsher than the other girls. We got plenty of whippings from "Deddy" (that is what we called him), and I guess because I was older, I got the worst of the beatings. That is what my young mind told me.

I wondered why I was the only one sent to spend the entire Sunday away from home with that lady and her sister to see the old ladies singing with other local singers. I would be gone all day, bored, with no one my age to talk to. That is why I do not mind being alone now. I also did not realize that was when I really began to favor gospel music over other music. Not all kinds of gospel, but the "hip-slapping" kind. I do remember being on a street that I thought was a long way from where we used to live, somewhere over on the other side of town. Through the years, I have been able to piece together some of what I should have known, but not all.

I wish I had known sooner after graduating from high school that I could have gone on to college instead of straight to New York. Overall, it was a valuable experience, though I still wish I had known all of my options. If I had, I could have made a different decision about the course of my life. Although, if I had taken another route, I would not have my children and they are my greatest gifts in life. Their dad knew the secret, but was forbidden to tell me. Damn, if we were right for each other, he would have told me. But we were not and I did not know the deep secret that had such a profound impact on my entire life.

What I did know, however, was there was a notable difference in my and my children's visual and physical health. I could not drive so I would take the bus to the babysitter's and then catch the bus back to the emergency room for treatment of their bronchial or asthma issues. My son had it worse than my daughter. Looking back, it's a shame the only time that little mean boy of mine gave us any peace was when he was sick. It would have been helpful to know why my children and I needed glasses while other siblings in the household had 20/20 vision. Eventually, I discovered that I had bronchial issues, pneumonia, and colds because my DNA was that of some other man and not MY DEDDY! There were so many notable signs, but it was after the fact that all things became one, and the whole assortment of problems were opened and revealed.

You could have told me in 1977, when your husband died, that someone else was my biological sperm donor. To find out almost 10 years later was mind-blowing! Who would have thought that there was a man, and at least four other siblings who looked just like me, or that I looked identical to them? The man too. I looked at his face in the hospital that day after all hell broke loose, and he looked at me. How could that be true? I grew up in the same household, and other than having many of the tougher-than-nail skills acquired during the years of my growth, I did not have a single commonality with them.

There was a sister about eleven months younger than me who looked like my identical twin. Yep, another sister, and a brother that I did not know, who passed before the huge revelation of all this. Then there was the brother, a career military officer, who came to our house plenty of times when I was a young girl. It was the craziest series of events. As mean as Deddy was, he never said anything disrespectful to the brother who was in the military, who always came to our house. It was not until the issue of my parentage and siblings was apparent to all of us that I put two and two together and realized that my brother was visiting to carry information back to his dad, who was also my dad. Funny thing, though, when I met my sister for the first time, I realized that the part of me that was lacking was her. Go figure. The most revealing of all of this was finally knowing why my vision was bad, and why my children and I had bronchial issues. There were plenty of health issues on that other side. The kids' dad always said, "That's from your side of the family." I wondered how that could be when everybody on my mother's side was perfectly fine with no health issues at all. Well, that's not entirely true because Deddy drank himself to death. I now understand why, but not until I was 35 years old!

So, here I am now at this ripe young-old age of seventy-two. Three of those four siblings that I did not get to know well have passed on into eternity. Only one of the siblings from the household in which I grew up has passed, and because he refused to quit smoking, he chose his own path leading to eternity. Yep, smoked until the day before his death, and drank beer too. Never had a cold or been sick a day in his 61 years of life.

I still wish I had known sooner so that I could have had a relationship with my biological dad. I could have chosen a different path in life. I could have been more keenly aware of the health issues my children and I had to encounter, or I would not have been so lonely growing up, or felt so out of place. I could actually wish that a lot of my life had been different, but my life was the one that I had. Just think, I have two sets of siblings, and not everyone can count that as a plus. The funny thing is, though, my children and I have the same characteristics as my biological father. Still, the tenacity that I have inherited from the Deddy who raised me is something for which I am eternally grateful. I could not have learned as much as I did had things been differently. I do not believe I would have had the fightback spirit I do.

Yeah, MAMA, you did a lot, but you chose the right path for me. You did not have to do it, but I am glad you did. Thank you for that. Thank you for your determined spirit. Thank you for that "I'm not going to let this defeat me attitude." Thank you for those things you told me, which made me wonder why. Thank you for being you!

Rest in Peace Mama……I will see you soon.

Daughter

"For His divine power has bestowed upon us all things that [are requisite and suited] to life and godliness, through the [[a]full, personal] knowledge of Him who called us by and to His own glory and excellence (virtue)." Peter 1:3 (AMPC)

Reflections

Use this space to write a memory, letter, or personal reflection.

"But they who wait for the LORD shall renew their strength; they shall mount up with wings like eagles; they shall run and not be weary, they shall walk and not faint." Isaiah 40:3

Inherited Legacy

Some of the greatest lessons in life aren't conveyed through lengthy conversations or detailed explanations. They are learned quietly, through keen observation of those who raise us. Growing up, she didn't always recognize the depth of her learning as she watched her mother—the strength she embodied, the decisions she made, and the way she navigated life with grace. Now, as a confident, independent woman, she clearly understands that many of the values and lessons she upholds today originated from her mother's example.

Hi Mom,

As I sit and write this letter, I'm thinking about all the life lessons I learned from you—some through direct guidance and others simply by watching how you moved through life. I also find myself reflecting on the things I have learned as a grown woman and sometimes wondering why you didn't share those experiences with me. Sometimes I even wonder if there were things you could have shared with me when I asked questions directly. Many times, the responses I received were short, indifferent, or not very transparent, and it made me wonder, "Why did I even ask Mom?" As I reflect more, I ask myself: How should I handle my mom's lack of transparency, vulnerability, and those tight lips when comfort is needed? Should I respond with annoyance or frustration? Instead, I choose to handle it with grace and the understanding that you have given me as much as you could based on your own experiences. For that, I say, "Thank you."

Mom, now at 53 years old and navigating this life of womanhood, adulthood, and motherhood, I can truly say you are my SHERO—the phenomenal woman you are.

I am because you were, and I am me because you are and continue to be.

Love you.

"Behold, everyone who uses proverbs will use this proverb about you: 'Like mother, like daughter.'" Ezekiel 16:44

Reflections

Use this space to write a memory, letter, or personal reflection.

____

____

____

____

____

____

____

____

____

____

____

____

____

____

____

____

____

"She is clothed with strength and dignity; she can laugh at the days to come. She speaks with wisdom, and faithful instruction is on her tongue." Proverbs 31:25-26 (NIV)

Unbracing My Past

I used to think that being a good daughter meant staying silent about the parts that hurt. But you can't heal what you don't acknowledge. This letter is a way of honoring her mother, while promising a different kind of safety for the children she may one day hold. This writer is on her way to acceptance and healing, trying to move forward without being held back by her past. Finding freedom from past burdens has helped to embrace new, more positive paths.

Dear Mom,

I've been thinking a lot lately about the way I was raised and how it influenced who I am today. There's something I've been meaning to say, not out of blame or bitterness, but out of honesty, reflection, and maybe even healing.

Growing up under your care taught me many lessons, some directly and others through contrast. I learned what love looks like in all its imperfect forms, and I also learned what I want to do differently if I ever have children of my own. There were moments when I carried the weight of expectations of holding the family together that I didn't understand. These experiences shaped me, not just in the ways that hurt, but in the clarity they've given me about the kind of environment I want to create for the next generation, should I choose to raise one.

If I have kids, I want them to feel safe. I want to create a space where they shouldn't have to be adults while still being children. A space where love isn't measured by just being strong to "get through it," but by understanding and consistency. I want to offer the kind of support I sometimes needed but didn't always know how to ask for.

None of this is to say you didn't try. I know you did what you could with what you had, your own past, your own struggles, your own version of love. And for all the ways you showed up, I'm grateful. This isn't about pointing fingers; it's about recognizing that cycles can continue, or they can shift, and I'm choosing the shift.

Thank you for the lessons, even the hard ones. They gave me the clarity I need to be the parent I hope to become, maybe one day. And those lessons also helped me better process my rearing, and you as a person beyond just the role of Mom.

With love

"This same God who takes care of me will supply all your needs from his glorious riches which have been given to us in Christ Jesus. Now glory be to God our father forever and ever. Amen." Philippians 4:19-20

Reflections

Use this space to write a memory, letter, or personal reflection.

"When I think of all this, I fall to my knees and I pray to the father, the creator of everything in heaven and on earth, I pray from his glorious unlimited resources he will empower you with inner strength through his spirit." Ephesians 3:14-18

Unveiled Peace

How does one summarize a lifetime of watching a giant walk among them? That is how the next daughter feels about her mother. Society has normalized the term "a product of our environment" as a negative connotation, but she embraces it differently. She is proud to be a product of her environment and considers herself the luckiest woman alive because her life was shaped entirely by her mother's strength, love, and prayers.

Dearest Mama,

Oh my God, where do I start?! First and foremost, I want to say "thank you" for just being who you are and have always been. I find it hard to adequately articulate just what I want to say because it's so much. As long as I can remember, you've been the "rock" of the family and the glue that binds us together. I can't ever remember a time when you weren't there, up until this day. When Daddy passed away when I was nine, you stepped right in and became the "quintessential" single parent. You continued to be there for your four girls, and even amid your grief, you never missed a beat.

My oldest siblings were already grown and out of the house, so that left sissy and me. Two years later, when sissy went to college, it was just you and me. I have so many memories of how you held it together, even though I had no idea the example you were setting for me at the time. The lessons were countless, and I still carry them with me to this day. You taught me that it was never too late to accomplish a dream or goal. After retiring from being a "domestic" by day and a custodian at night for 27 years, you immediately went back to college for eight straight years. You started college in the '50s but gave it up to both start and help raise a family. When it was all said and done, you obtained your Doctorate in Christian Psychology at 61 years old! That's just one of the many examples that helped to mold me into the woman that I've become. Your strength over the years continues to leave me in awe. You became a widow at an early age, and last year at 91 years old, you outlived one of your daughters. Yet, once again while grieving, you immediately started giving God praise. I was in awe that at one of the most painful times in your life, you chose to praise God. I've always said that "at the end of my life, if I could be a third of the woman my Mama was, that I would have accomplished much." That's how much you mean to me.

Your Daughter

"Cast your burden on the Lord [releasing the weight of it] and He will sustain you; He will never allow the [consistently] righteous to be moved (made to slip, fall, or fail)." Psalm 55:22 (AMPC)

Reflections

Use this space to write a memory, letter, or personal reflection.

"Surely you have heard about the administration of God's grace that was given to me for you." Ephesians 3:2 (NIV)

Before I Forget Me

A mother is preemptively apologizing to her daughter for the care she believes may eventually cause her daughter stress. She wants her daughter to understand that it is perfectly okay if she needs to make alternative arrangements for her steady decline. She wants her daughter to live her life freely, without feeling burdened. Is this request even possible?

Dearest Daughter,

I write because these thoughts are often too difficult to speak through tears. I have been battling cognitive changes that frighten me. I guess that is what they call dementia or Alzheimer's these days. I never asked too much of you and I'm sorry that I must now. The one promise that I need from you is to let nothing break our bond, not even me.

Please research and arm yourself with the knowledge of how. Understanding what lies ahead is important for both of us. I may forget names or details of our lives, but do not let frustration take hold. These lapses are symptoms of my condition, not a loss of love.

I apologize now for the times I may become a burden to you. While specific details may blur, the thought of you is still. Remind me of us! The joy and the challenges.

This journey will take a toll on you. It is natural to feel anger and sadness, but please do not shoulder these emotions alone. Use your circle and prioritize your well-being. If the day comes when my needs exceed what you can or are willing to provide, I give you my blessing to seek outside care and not feel bad about it.

I am sharing this now because I believe in your strength.

Love,
Mum

When life gets too hard to stand, kneel and find your strength, your faith, and your will to EVERYTHING!

Reflections

Use this space to write a memory, letter, or personal reflection.

"I love you, Lord, you are my strength. The Lord is my rock, my fortress, and my savior. My God is my rock in whom I find protection, he is my shield, the power that saves me, and my place of safety. I call on the Lord, who is worthy of praise, and he saved me from my enemies." PSALM 18:1-3

Breaking the Silence

In this letter, a mother reflects on her daughter's coming out, expressing a complex mix of pride, love, internal conflict, and regret. She acknowledges moments where she fell short—particularly in not fully supporting her daughter during a difficult family exchange— while also grappling with her own beliefs and past influences. Through honesty and vulnerability, she reveals the lasting impact of their separation and her ongoing grief. The letter ultimately conveys enduring love and a desire for reconciliation, growth, and understanding despite their differences.

Dear Daughter,

Having you and your brothers has been the greatest joy of my life. When the doctor told me I was having a girl, I was especially excited about having you. I had been waiting for a little girl.

I will never forget the day you came to your father and me privately, without your brothers. You professed to us that you were gay and that you were ready to date. You even wanted to invite a friend over for dinner. I must admit, I felt relieved that my daughter chose to confide in us. There are times when matters like these could have a much different outcome. I was proud, and it reassured me that all my time, prayers, and hard work was not in vain. However, I must also admit that I was a little embarrassed to have a daughter who was gay.

We all have our flaws, and I choose my battles wisely, with God always on my side. I hope you know that I love and support you, but that doesn't mean I agree with all your actions. That is a natural part of any relationship.

When your father started crying and ranting during our conversation, I knew it confused you even more. I'm sorry I didn't speak up for you during that moment. He suggested you try dating young men first. He believed you couldn't claim to be gay until you had at least had a heterosexual dating experience. To be honest, I secretly hoped you would also give dating a young man a chance.

I was ready to walk away from your father when you began crying uncontrollably and apologizing for disappointing us. You did not let us down at all. When parents have dreams for their children, those are our dreams, not yours. It's unfair for a parent to impose their dreams on their children. I should know this better than anyone. My mother did the exact same thing for years. If I did that to you unknowingly, I am sorry.

I want to remind you that the Bible guides us on how to live our lives day by day. You were raised with strong morals, and I was hoping you could stand by them. Even when you think no one is watching, God always is.

There's something personal I want to share that has hurt our family for too long. Your father had a brother who was gay. He was bullied in school, and your dad often had to defend him, even though he was the youngest and felt embarrassed by it. In a way, your dad was his biggest bully, even if he never realized it. Even though I may disagree with your lifestyle, I will still support you because you are my baby girl, and I love you.

I wonder if knowing about your uncle would have made it easier for you to handle your father's reaction or anyone else's response to your chosen lifestyle. I forgive you for leaving me to mourn after you left us. Your father couldn't take it anymore, and now, I cry for him too. I am here alone, grieving the both of you.

Your brothers are both married with children. They check on their mother. Don't you worry, I keep plenty busy. And yes, I still drive. I spend my days volunteering with parents in the LGBT community because I understand the pain. I want to help others because I miss my baby girl every day. Sharing our story is essential for me. I remember you saying you wanted to be a teacher; well, I'm teaching MOTHERS AND FATHERS how to accept, even when they disagree. I pray that you forgave me. I love you so much!

Always,

Your Mother

"Be careful, our hearts will be weighed down with carousing, drunkenness, and the anxieties of life, and that day will close on you suddenly like a trap." Luke 21:34

Reflections

Use this space to write a memory, letter, or personal reflection.

"But they who wait for the Lord shall renew their strength; they shall mount up with wings like eagles; they shall run and not be weary; they shall walk and not faint." Isaiah 40:31

Enough!

This is going to be a lengthy letter, and I already feel that writing it will bring tears to my eyes. I plan to share it with my husband just to make sure I am not being unfair to my mother with my words. I have also told my brothers that I am writing this letter to her, hoping to get confirmation from them that it's okay to voice these feelings. It's important to me to have their support since I understand how sensitive our family dynamics can be, especially considering our family traditions and expectations.

I want to tread carefully on this topic because I know how deeply generational curses can scar a parent-child relationship. Although it's always a challenge, I still want to show you some respect, even when you don't deserve it.

I discussed with my stepdad how you treated me throughout the years, and he admitted he was aware of it. He indicated that he wanted all the kids to be alright before he made the decision to leave you. I want you to know that I never wished for that separation; it made me feel terrible and left me confused about where I stood. He tried to explain why certain situations unfolded as they did in our family, but this pain is real, and it hurts like hell. Everyone, including my stepdad, encouraged me to mail this letter, saying it might help me feel better. Yet, I still couldn't bring myself to do it.

It's not that I think it would hurt your feelings—though it might. I've pondered on the idea that if you received this letter sharing my truth, and you didn't come rushing over to talk, to apologize, to hug me, I don't know if I could cope with that emotional abandonment yet again. The potential pain of that is overwhelming, which is one of the reasons I've hesitated to express these feelings fully.

The last few times I have attempted to talk to you, I ended up in tears. It has become incredibly difficult to articulate the emotions I carry without feeling like I'm being dismissed or invalidated. I have so many issues I've tried to address with you over the years, but they have often been met with silence or indifference on your part. The emotional neglect is something you don't seem to acknowledge or care about, which is painful. Now, as a mother myself, I find myself having to dig deep to show my daughter love and affection. Sometimes, it is a bit draining, and I struggle with the vulnerability that comes with it.

I vow to never call her out of her name like you did to me, and it's disheartening that she has heard you refer to people with disabilities as "retarded." That word stings deeply because I am disabled, and I have endured it myself. Your words have left scars on my soul and spirit, making it even more important for me to change how I communicate with my daughter. This cycle of emotional abuse and neglect ends here.

You never believed me when I confided in you about Papi's friends messing with me whenever he came to our house. Instead of confronting him, you accused me of being "fast." No! You were the fast ass! I saw you and Papi's friend. I try to work through all this bullshit, and not harbor hatred towards you, but it's hard when I feel like I've been treated like I'm the worst person in the world.

You knew my uncle was a pedophile. The fear and anguish that surrounded that chapter of my life were crushing, and you, along with everyone else, intimidated me into silence. After a friend told our school counselor what I told him, you said I was lying. I do not know if I can ever forget that. Or if I even want to.

In our old house, you were aware that my bedroom was moldy when we moved in, yet we stayed. Another poor mom decision that caused me to develop asthma. Of course, it was easy for you to ignore that important factor. I understood there were financial challenges, and I sympathize with those struggles, but all the emotional toil caused by you remains, and so does my asthma. It feels like the pain from those experiences is stuck in my body, reminding me of past neglect.

Going to the doctor was always a source of anxiety. If I needed any medication, you would place the blame solely on me. When the dentist informed you that I needed braces, it was the end of the world. I remember vividly how everyone else received what they wanted for Christmas that year, except for me. I received clothes that year. You said my gifts were in my mouth. It was during that time that I learned to bottle my feelings and keep them to myself. I began to pretend that I was an only child to cope with the loneliness. I secretly hated my siblings back then.

That pretense lasted until one day when my stepbrother and I were arguing over hair I left in the shower. You walked in, and without asking for my side of the story, you immediately took his side. You didn't show any care for my feelings or my tears, which made me feel invisible. This experience solidified what I had always told myself, that I would leave as soon as I graduated high school.

Instead of having meaningful conversations with me, you often spoke at me, especially when you were angry. You would complain that I looked just like Papi, and sometimes I caught you staring at me, only for that gaze to turn into frustration. You didn't think I noticed, did you? It became clear to me over time that your anger and disappointment stemmed from my resemblance to him. But I am my own person—I am not him.

I still don't understand why you struggled to be a mother to me when you had a good childhood with your sisters and some of your brothers. What went wrong? Why couldn't I have a normal mother-daughter relationship? It feels like a dark hole where love and understanding should have existed.

Now, in adulthood, forming any kind of relationship with you is still a work in progress. I want to learn to trust you with my children, but we need to start sorting through some issues in our relationship first. It's crucial that we acknowledge and address the issues I have laid out. That is the only way to begin the long road ahead of us.

An apology would certainly help, but I want it to come from you, and in your own time. I need it to be sincere. I want to understand who you are. I don't know much beyond you being my mother. In turn, I suspect you do not know the woman I am becoming. I want to connect, to share who I am with you beyond the surface and our past experiences.

Currently, I see a therapist every week because my anxiety is through the roof, and I've lost hair due to stress. I thought it would be a good time for us to meet, especially after the family reunion. However, I tried to speak with you, only you ignored me entirely. That silence stung, leaving me feeling lost and alone in a room full of family.

Somehow, it got back to you that I complained about your narcissistic tendencies. At this point, I do not feel guilty about expressing my feelings. You have had more than enough time to address our issues, and what I feel now is abandonment.

I chose to block you on social media, and I found it necessary. Seeing your posts about visiting my brother was the last straw for me; it seemed like you were deliberately trying to hurt me by flaunting your connection with him. It felt malicious and petty, and I simply cannot continue to allow myself to be drawn into that sort of emotional turmoil.

You appear to be living your best life, enjoying everything it has to offer, while I'm stuck in the same place emotionally. It's becoming clear to me that the gap between us may be too wide to bridge at this point. It might be best for both of us to keep things as they are for now, so I can focus on my own healing without feeling obligated to mend our strained relationship immediately.

Trying not to feel bitter or angry is almost impossible when reflecting on everything I've gone through. A year ago, I had arranged flowers to be delivered to your workplace, hoping to reconnect. I invited you to meet me at Starbucks, but you never showed up. Why didn't you come? Your absence was a clear signal that the distance between us was still very much there, and that you try to act as if you were unaware of or unwilling to deal with our issues truly.

I had hoped the flowers might show you my desire to mend our relationship, but the lack of response was devastating. You knew even then that I was prepared to put you out of my life if necessary. That realization has left me feeling empty inside.

This may come off as like all I'm doing now is venting complaints, but I am done with that part. I am trying to sort through my own stuff without having to deal with yours and it is already more than I can handle. I didn't choose this path, nor did I choose the conditions that have led me here.

I want you to understand that, in many ways, I've moved on. I am starting a new life for myself and my daughter—one that I pray will be filled with love, understanding, and emotional connection. My goal is to ensure that my daughter never feels the weight of parental neglect in the way that I did.

I hope this letter helps answer any questions you may have about my feelings for you. I want both of us to try and understand one another's fears. It's my deepest wish that we can begin to mend the unfortunate reality we've found ourselves in.

I would like a chance to heal and create a new narrative for our relationship —one based on honesty and respect. I hope we can find common ground and move forward toward a brighter, more hopeful future together. Thank you for reading this. I look forward to your thoughts whenever you feel ready to share them.

I love you.

PS...

If only I had the courage to mail this!

"Rejoice always, pray continually, give thanks in all circumstances; for this is God's will for you in Christ Jesus." 1 Thessalonians 5:16-18 (NIV)

Reflections

Use this space to write a memory, letter, or personal reflection.

Enough!

"Better a patient person than a warrior, one with self-control than one who takes a city." Proverbs 16:32 (NIV)

Unrecognizable

It's been quite some time since a daughter has spent quality time with her mother. Now that she has her own family, the yearning to rekindle her bond with her mother becomes increasingly stronger. When losing someone tears a family apart, the loss can cause deeper issues to unfold. Looking ahead, we'll experience a rich tapestry of emotions: anger, disgust, fear, happiness, sadness, surprise, and contempt. By recognizing and embracing these feelings, we can navigate life's events with greater understanding and resilience. Let's journey through this emotional landscape together!

Mom,

It has been at least ten years since I've last seen you. At that time, I was pregnant with my first child, and now I also have a four-year-old. You have no idea how many times I looked for you—on Facebook, through obituaries, and even by going back to the place you were born. My last resort was the morgue. Then eventually, I decided that I did not care if I ever saw you again. The strange thing is, I was never prepared for what I would do if I actually found you.

One day, after a year of accepting that I would never hear from or see you again, I received a friend request from someone with your name. I knew there was no way the person in the profile photo could not be my mother. Anger consumed my emotions for the rest of that day. While I was relieved to know you were alive, seeing what you looked like now filled me with disgust. I didn't know whether to cry in sadness or be angry with you. It was clear that you had chosen drugs over your children and grandchildren. I hate that I am even crying as I write this. I don't want to waste tears on you anymore. You were my best friend for a long time when I was growing up. Now that I'm older and have my own children, I realize that my siblings and I needed our mother to raise us, not be our friend.

After my brother died, you forgot about the three children who still needed you. I do not know what you were going through, but we all were grieving the loss of my brother, too. You allowed Child Protective Services to remove my only remaining brothers from what they knew as home, and you did not care. I was left to fend for myself because of my age. Have you reached out to them at all over the years? They deserved so much better than you and what you gave them. We all did.

Heroin and crack destroyed our family. The beautiful woman and mother we once knew is now a stranger to me. I've been too afraid to reach out to you to introduce you to your grandchildren, because if you relapse, my anger would turn to hate. I do not want to bring that to my family. EVER! My kids would never get to know you if you did that. You will not mentally fuck them the same way you did me. I often wondered, as a stranger, if you could have loved me better. Why wasn't I enough?

That's a fucking question, MOM!

"If anyone is in Christ, he is a new creation; the old has gone, the new has come!" 2 Corinthians 5:17 (NLT)

Reflections

Use this space to write a memory, letter, or personal reflection.

"The Lord is faithful to all His promises and loving towards all he has made." Psalm 145:13 (NLT)

Loving You through a New Lens

Healing is rarely a straight line. For this writer, it was a path that led through years of loneliness, fractured sisterhood, and the discovery of a mother's hidden trauma. In this vulnerable reflection, she shares how counseling and faith allowed her to stop dwelling on the past and instead start creating a future that honors a complicated memory. What follows is a narrative of survival, discovery, and the power of forgiveness.

Hi Mother,

Growing up in a house with you was not easy. Watching what you put my two older sisters through allowed me to attain some wisdom. You treated my older sister very harshly and my middle sister like a spoiled kid handled with gloves. Of course, this was from my perspective. Then there was me. One would think being the baby meant I would have the best of everything, but that wasn't the case for me. I felt more like an afterthought and often felt excluded and alone.

I felt sorry for my older sister and resented my middle sister because of the way you treated them. If "oh yeah, the other one" was a person, I would be its twin. There were times I longed for attention and didn't get it. We all have different fathers and my sisters' fathers were active in their lives, and it bothered me that mine was not. This made the loneliness even more intense. I bonded with my grandmother but still longed for attention from my parents.

Instability was the norm for us. Our early years were with my grandmother and when I was around five years old, you finally got a place of your own. This meant my sisters and I no longer had the protection provided by our grandmother's interference when you were abusive. From the time I was in 5th grade until 7th grade, we were pretty much homeless. My older sisters stayed with our grandmother who already had a house full. For some reason, I stayed with you, and we literally lived from pillow to post. Finally, by the 8th grade, you found a place for us all to stay again.

My sisters and I witnessed you use drugs, and be used and abused by men. You allowed different men in our homes on a regular. We never moved in with any of them, but they were always moving in with us. When things were good with the men, things were good at the house. When things went bad, it was bad for us. Instead of getting closer, we were divided. The relationships between my sisters and me are still strained because of the things we endured growing up.

Despite everything, you did try to be active in our lives. You loved God and kept us in church. You never had much, but would give your last to anyone. It was almost like you were two different people. You would be up for a minute and out of the blue, you'd then be down. The mood swings and frequent outbursts of anger were, at times, difficult to process and manage–especially for little children.

It wasn't until after I was grown and had a family of my own, that I learned you were molested and raped as a child and adolescent, and also suffered from mental illness. You had even been hospitalized twice as a child as a result. You wouldn't allow us to get very close to you and never told us you loved us. After learning this information, I began to have empathy for you. I realized you were trying to navigate through life while hurting. I also realized life wasn't easy for you growing up and you were only doing the best you could with the knowledge you had.

Knowledge is power and from that point on, I began to love you despite all that you had done and all that I endured. My faith in God grew and I started counseling because breaking that spiritual curse was mandatory. December 16th will be six years since we lost you, and I miss you like it was yesterday. I wish I had had more time to love you. I do not dwell on the past, but I try to create a future that includes you and the memory of you.

Love you always!
Your Daughter

"His divine power has given us everything we need for a godly life through our knowledge of him who called us by his own glory and goodness. Through these, he has given us his very great and precious promises, so that through them you may participate in the divine nature, having escaped the corruption in the world caused by evil desires." 2 Peter 1:3-4

Reflections

Use this space to write a memory, letter, or personal reflection.

"Grace and peace be yours in abundance through the knowledge of God and of Jesus our Lord." 2 Peter 1:2

My Keys Lead to Peace

In this letter, a daughter reflects on growing up under a strict and protective mother, which made it difficult for her to express herself and seek emotional support. She shares pivotal moments from her adolescence and adulthood that left lasting emotional wounds, including experiences of fear, silence, and unmet needs. Though she acknowledges her love for her mother, she reveals unresolved pain and the boundaries she has established to protect herself. The letter offers a poignant look at how unspoken hurt can shape a relationship over time.

I was 13 years old. My body matured quicker than my age, which attracted the attention of older men. My mom would often tell them, "She is only 13 years old." Their response was usually, "WOW!" I believe that was the beginning of many challenges for me. My mom was very protective of her daughters. We couldn't talk to men, not even teenage males that were our age. We often got into trouble because of how protective she was of us, which made it difficult for me to express myself to her. Anytime I built up enough courage to do so, I became anxious about the way she would respond.

When I turned 15, I met my son's father. We started as friends, but our relationship quickly evolved beyond friendship. Soon after, I discovered I was pregnant after losing my virginity to him, and I had no idea what to do or how to tell my mom. I started wearing bigger clothes, and I avoided her as much as possible. I tried to hide it for at least six months before finally confessing. I was afraid of what her reaction would be, but she was very direct when she spoke to us.

I knew that my past would affect me, and even today, I still sometimes struggle to express my true feelings to others. For example, when I bought my house, I did not tell my mom. Instead, I decided to surprise her. When she first saw it, her response was that it was an ugly house. That hurt my feelings so deeply that I just cried. Another incident occurred after I bought the house. I found myself in an unfortunate predicament without any food and was very hungry. I went to my mom's house to ask for some food, knowing her deep freezer was always full and her pantry overflowing. She told me she had just given three bags of food to one of my sisters for her and her children. I walked out of the house crying because I expected her to say, "Go get what you want." For over twenty years, I kept this hurt in my heart without ever telling my mom how much it affected me, and I never forgave her for it. Even to this day, I have never asked her for anything. My mother still does not realize how deeply she hurt me. And she never will. I love my mother, but I have established clear boundaries that I will not allow her to push past.

A daughter

"But seek first the kingdom of God and His righteousness, and all these things will be added unto you." Matthew 6:33

Reflections

Use this space to write a memory, letter, or personal reflection.

____

____

____

____

____

____

____

____

____

____

____

____

____

____

____

____

____

"...a man's enemies will be the members of his own household. Anyone who loves their father or mother more than me is not worthy of me..." Matthew 10:36–37 (NIV)

Sticks and Stones

"I really hate my mom! I never want to speak to you again. As soon as I am old enough, I'm leaving." Have you ever felt this way or said those words to yourself? Raised by her grandmother, our next writer knows abandonment and shame all too well. After her mother moved to another country to be with a man she met online, visits became shorter and less frequent over the years. So, too, did the love she had for her mother.

Ma,

Your strictness and harshness scared me. I could not pretend to love you as if my feelings didn't matter. I often heard you praise the beauty of my sister and cousins so often that I lost count. Was it because they were lighter and thinner? Those were your standards, not mine; yet your constant criticism and comparisons eroded every bit of self-esteem I tried to build. I never understood why it was so difficult for you to tell me I was beautiful, too.

Now that I am an adult, nothing has changed. I overheard my grandmother say, "You look just like your father," and suddenly, I am being compared to my dad with comments about how "masculine" my shoulders and hands are. You leave me feeling insecure and drained every time I am in your presence.

The relationship you share with my brother and sister is hurtful to me. You give them love and kindness while treating me like an outsider. Why do you call me "weak" instead of offering encouragement? Is it because I stood up for myself while everyone else lets you say whatever comes to your mind? The only praise you ever gave me was for a success you could brag about or financial gains, as if that is the only value I have to offer. And if I'm being completely honest, the only thing you ever gave me was a reason to leave. I am finally old enough. I am finally strong enough. And I have finally had enough. Consider this my last everything!

Goodbye

"And God will wipe away every tear from their eyes; there shall be no more death, nor sorrow, nor crying. There shall be no more pain, for the former things have passed away." Revelation 21:4 (NKJV)

Reflections

Use this space to write a memory, letter, or personal reflection.

____

____

____

____

____

____

____

____

____

____

____

____

____

____

____

____

____

Mark 5:26 describes the desperate situation of a woman who had been suffering from a chronic hemorrhage (bleeding) for twelve years.

A Trilogy of Truth

This "Trilogy of Truth" weaves together deeply personal reflections from multiple generations within one family, revealing the complexities of love, absence, and identity. Through a daughter's honest moment of vulnerability with her mother to the confrontation of her father's absence, plus her brother's heartfelt apology to his grandmother, each piece uncovers unspoken emotions that have shaped their lives. Together, their voices highlight both the fractures and the resilience within familial bonds. The collection ultimately speaks to healing, accountability, and the enduring power of love across generations.

Dear Sweet Butterfly

In the quiet morning light, a mother's love unfolds.
I look into your eyes with a gentle gaze and see all that you carry.
From whispered dreams in the middle of the night
to every fear you softened and held for me.

We grew like rivers branching free.
You were my anchor, and somehow, also me.
Your love was loud, unafraid to be seen,
yet stitched into the smallest moments
brushed hair, warm meals, steady hands.

I watched you break and still rebuild yourself from nothing.
There were seasons of distance—
doors closing a little harder,
words cutting a little deeper,
Love is sometimes lost in translation.

Still, you shaped me,
teaching me how to hold the weight of the world.

Even as we grew apart into our own lives,
There was always an invisible thread.
Unbroken, unwavering,
pulling us gently, heart to heart.

I practiced the words in pieces,
like lines from a favorite movie,
repeating them until they almost felt like mine.

"Mom, I need to tell you something…"

But you were in the kitchen, like always
Hands busy, heart open.
The truth sat heavily in my chest.
I imagined all the ways it could break us.

Then you looked at me
those concerned eyes,
that voice that taught me bravery
before I even knew fear.

So I said it.
Not perfectly, not rehearsed
just real.

"Mom… I like girls."

The world paused
Or maybe it was just me,
waiting for something to shatter.

You cried.
You looked at me with heartbreak and disbelief.
But your arms still knew how to hold me,
And your voice didn't tremble when you said my name.

It took years, even
for us to find our way back,
to rebuild what felt fragile.

But the truth didn't break us.
It brought me back to you
fully, finally, without hiding.

And I realized then:

I was never stepping away from your love.
I was stepping into it myself.

ME

Daddy's Little Girl

I used to fit in your arms
like I was made for that exact space
My small hand wrapped around your finger,
trusting you to hold my whole world steady.

You called me your little girl
like it was a promise,
like no matter how tall I grew
or how far I wandered,
I would always have a place beside you.

I think you loved me enough to hold on
and loved me even more to let me go.

Now I see you in quieter ways
In a strength I didn't know I borrowed,
in courage that feels like you,
in the calm that comes

when I hear your voice in my head.

I'm not that little anymore.
My world no longer fits inside your arms,
But somehow your love still does.

And I'll always be your little girl
not because I never grew up,
but because you never stopped
looking at me
like I was something to protect,
something to believe in,
something you would choose
over and over again.

There's a space in my preteen years
in milestones and memories
where your absence was loud,
painted vividly in my mind.

I wanted to see you,
to hear you say you were proud of me
after awards days and small victories.

You were there for my high school graduation,
a huge milestone,
But so many others
were met with silence.

Not loud or angry
just missing.

Like a chair no one sits in,
a name that feels unfamiliar
on your own lips.

But my life didn't stop
to wait for you.

My mom became everything
soft when the world was hard,
strong when it tried to break me.

Two hands doing the work of four,
a heart stretching past its limits
just to make sure mine stayed whole.

And look at me
growing in the absence,
not defined by it,
but shaped into something
fierce and tender all at once.

I was never abandoned by love.
It found me anyway.
in unstoppable form,
in the woman who stayed,
who chose me every single day,
who filled the silence you left
with something so full
it echoed.

Then we found our way back
in my early twenties,
like I had known you every day
even when I hadn't.

Time had done its quiet work
etched years into your face,
into mine
a history we didn't share
but somehow still carried.

In every pause,
every glance that lingered too long,
every almost-apology
caught in your throat.

There's no map for this.
for rebuilding something
That should never have broken.

Only patience.
Only the courage to stay.

You told me you thought of me
in ordinary moments,
in things that reminded you
of the life you stepped away from.

You said you left
because things were hard
between you and Mom.

And I wanted to be angry.
Maybe I was.
Maybe part of me still is.

So I let you in
not all at once,
but piece by piece,
like a door opening just enough
for the light to enter.

You were always the more understanding one
the parent who listened,
who spoke without judgment.

And there we were,
learning each other
in the present tense,
you choosing finally
to be part of my story.

Maybe that's what healing looks like:
not erasing the distance,
not pretending it didn't hurt,
but reaching across it anyway.

Dad, I forgive you.

But I will never forget
the milestones you missed,
the moments you should have been there
physically, mentally, emotionally
as my father.

And still...
I am,
and will always be
Your little girl.

Me

In **Mother May I**, we saw the daughter's ache. In the forthcoming sequel, **Beyond the Barbershop: Stuff Men Won't Talk About**, we'll hear the men finally speak. The next letter is a sneak peek of what's to come when men finally break the silence.

The author honors his grandmother with deep gratitude. By finally speaking to the matriarch, he breaks the cycle of silence, revealing the "stuff men won't say" about the fathers who left and the women who stayed to pick up the pieces.

Grandma,

I want to begin this letter by expressing my heartfelt apologies. You did your absolute best in raising twelve children, but I know it was hard because of the circumstances that unfolded. All twelve children graduated from high school, yet many struggled in life due to poor choices. Among them was your eldest child, who fathered a child with a woman who, unfortunately, was not and still isn't the most supportive or a positive influence.

I'm especially sorry that you had to step in and raise me, your seventh son, thirteenth child, and fourth grandchild. Not once did you complain or make me feel like a burden. I know in my heart that you provided me with a better life than most in my situation could hope for. You embraced your role as my guardian with grace and unwavering dedication, never faltering in your commitment. Day in and day out, you gave your all.

I apologize for the fact that you spent much of your life caring for children. I'm sorry for any disappointment you felt in a son you hoped would become a responsible man, one who would provide for his child as you did for him. I regret that he missed birthdays, plays, major holidays, my first dance, and moments with his grandchildren. I'm sorry he chose alcohol over family. And let's not overlook the mother of his child, who claimed to be wonderful but fell short.

I apologize for holding in so many emotions due to the physical and mental abuse from my own mother. While she may be my biological parent, you were the one to nurture and prepare me for what life would offer.

I regret the years that have passed since I left home, during which you faced immense pain and suffering from those who should have cared for you. Knowing you suffered before dying is unbearable, and the memory of April 8th will forever be etched in my mind. I wish I could have made choices for you, but I assured you I would never return to that place of torment. For a long time, I clung to anger, convinced that they had taken you from me. I realize now how much that animosity would upset you. Please accept my heartfelt apologies for holding on to such bitterness.

I love you, Grandma.

Conclusion

Dear Mothers,

We cannot love our daughters in their twenties the same way we loved them as a baby. As our daughters mature into adulthood and navigate new challenges and experiences, our love must evolve alongside theirs. As newborns, our passion was nurturing, filled with bedtime stories, love, and kisses. By 10, it shifted to encouragement, celebrating her milestones in school sports, cheering her on, and helping her build friendships. At 15, our love became a battle (excuse me–grab your pearls) over guidance and independence, as she developed her individuality while still providing a safety net. Now, at 21, our relationship demands a deeper connection grounded in mutual respect, trust, understanding, and support for her goals and aspirations.

New Stage: I'M GROWN

They can't wait to say that! Do they not know that's an unwritten rule that's disrespectful to say to your mom? We know! We don't want to hear it all the time. Just don't get too grown to call your mother when you need her.

I pray for those who never knew this kind of love and encouragement. Some women believe they have healed from past trauma, but in reality, they don't have an ounce of peace. We often disguise a pretty, beat face, high-paying jobs as our peace, or at least that's what the perfect posed picture on Facebook displays for everyone.

We sometimes suffer in silence because we bear the title "mother." Pausing for the cause does not always work for us, unless it involves the ambulance or an extended stay at the hospital. We must find strength in the midst of our storm because we are mothers, because they are ours, and because their eyes are watching us. As much as we love our daughters, it is imperative that we first teach them to love the Lord, so that when they encounter life's challenges, they can rely on their faith to see them through.

Dear Daughters,

Together, we can break the cycle of silence and trauma, creating a legacy of love that lasts for generations to come.

You will experience failures, wins, losses, and changes. You will face obstacles to forge through, and through it all, you will become even stronger than you could have imagined. My prayer is that you meet the world with your head held high and your shoulders back (**let them see you coming**). Always give yourself grace and never forget the strength that is already woven into who you are.

Wherever you decide to go, my love will be with you. Whatever you choose to do in life, my pride in you never fades. And whoever you choose to become, you will always be enough, worthy, and uniquely our daughter.

There aren't any manuals provided for mothers to help us become better; we can only pray and trust that the Lord will continue to bless us by watching over our daughters. The relationship between a mother and daughter is a powerful bond; yet it can also be one of the most difficult because conversations never had can turn into silent walls.

Talk to your mom. Allow her to **<u>GROW</u>** through it with you. This will help us gain a better understanding of you and your experiences. It is never too late to express what and how you feel.

Moving Forward

If you are here, it's because you know the weight of the "silent war." It's the tension that hangs in the air during holiday dinners, the phone calls that feel like minefields, and the unspoken words that stretch the distance between a mother's heart and a daughter's life.

Mother May I-With All Due Respect was written to give voice to the feelings we've tucked away to keep the peace. But a book is just the beginning. Real healing happens when we move from reading to *relating*.

Strong Woman:
A Poem Every Mother and Daughter Should Hear

I like you – You Strong Woman!
Determined and true
So focused are you
Your strength on display
Never let them take that away
It's also your meekness
That many mistake for a weakness
You just appear vulnerable from the start
Because of the size of your heart

I respect you-You Strong Woman!
Sometimes stepping from the back
To take the brunt of the impact
Sometimes stepping behind
Giving that silent support sublime
Trying to like this man
That you worked hard to understand
Trying to help this child
To whom you've gone the last mile

I admire you-You strong Woman!
As proud as you want to be
Each day of your existence
is a lifetime's legacy
Senses are tested not just with the eyes
Deep in your soul lies the real prize
You stand among the tested with superb grace
You lie among the honored in your rightful place

I adore you-You Strong Woman!
Always giving and trusting to the extreme
Supporting and caring
Character of gender supreme
You come in many packages
You may vary in style
But you all have the strength
To go the last mile

I love you-You Strong Woman!
I see you everywhere
Your presence and beauty beyond compare
That radiant charm
Those lovely arms
It's in your dance
Bringing tender visions of romance
It's in your talk
And that proud steady walk
No memories needed
I know it now
So humbly Strong Woman
I gracefully bow

Strong Woman!

I Like You!
I Respect You!
I Admire You!
I Adore You!
I Love You!

©Written   and   Composed   by   Jackie   Robinson   7/23/98

Who I Am

Often, the most difficult thing for each of us to see

Is the answer to the personal question, "How to just be me?"

As we walk the road of self-support in this land of liberty

There's only one way that each of us can truly be "totally" free

Regardless of all the challenges of life, which vary for each of our destiny

The result should be "I did my best and I'm OK," and that's all you need to be

The mistake that many of us make, as each situation arise

Is we try to fit in and be accepted, and hope never to be despised

The ultimate hope and end pursued, regardless of the organization

Is to enhance its existence and maintain its purpose when we serve in a station

As we have the opportunity to be effective when presented a situation

So many of us want to be accepted and received, and be treated with total elation

So we bask in the environment of being held in wonder and personally idolized

And happily sail the wave of special attention and the self-aggrandizement ride

We welcome those who will fuel our tank, for a moment of personal attention

We will scorn the one who is not in awe, as our status or name is mentioned

It should all be the work, the achievement, and the contribution while having a dose of fun

It should not be a painful trip or at the expense of anyone

And the end should be, "look at us and what we did together"

And we accomplished this result, in all kinds of storms and weather

Then, why do we treat one with suspicion, if they are not our clone or what we feel is Ok

As if someone made our mold, the "perfect one," and threw the design away

So do not look for someone to proclaim themselves an expert on YOU and eventually say

I've thought about it and decided that you are alright, and therefore you can stay

Jackie Roberson © 2012

MMI: Updates

A little over a year ago, I conducted research in preparation for **Mother May I** and received occasional updates throughout the year from the contributors who significantly enriched this book. Some of those updates that I've received since the original letters were drafted are described below.

1,206 Seconds of New Energy

In January 2026, less than a year after the letter was written and mailed, her mother passed away. Writing those words hadn't just been an exercise in release; it led to mending and healing while there was still time.

In her mother's final hours, the doctors informed the family that her bodily functions were failing, and she was no longer able to respond. As she lay crying on her mother's chest, a lifetime of "silent wars" finally broke through, prompting her to whisper a question she knew wouldn't be answered: "Do you know how much I'm going to miss you, Mama?"

In that moment, her mother didn't just seem to hear her—she answered. With the last of her strength, she kicked her husband's hand and spoke one final, clear word: "Yeah."

They stayed by her side until the very end. Because she had chosen to write that letter, she didn't have to say goodbye to a stranger or an adversary. Instead, she could say goodbye to her mother, knowing that they were both finally at peace together.

I Wasn't Ready

Since the final chapters of *Mother May I* were written, a significant shift occurred in this family's journey. The grandmother has been granted full legal custody of her granddaughter.

Now that she has the responsibility of the next generation, her focus remains steadfast on building a bridge back to her daughter. She continues to reach out, with hopes of a restored relationship rooted in mutual respect and greater intention. They are walking a path of healing—one guided by the belief that grace can eventually lead even the most fractured hearts back to one another.

Deep Seated Dependency

In her last letter, she spoke openly about the "double-edged sword" of independence—the thin line between the strength she found after her mother's passing and the quiet loneliness that often followed. It was a period of deep reflection, marked by the weight of standing on her own for the first time.

Today, that landscape has shifted.

Since moving, the author has stepped into a new season of life. While that independence remains her foundation, it is no longer a solitary burden. She is now surrounded by family and the fresh energy of new friendships.

This move represents more than just a change in address; it is a shift in perspective. She discovers that true independence doesn't mean being alone; it means having the freedom to build a life where she is supported, seen, and finally, at home.

Same Daughter, Newer Truth

"Mask," she said. Her mother acknowledged with a nod and silence filled the room. The daughter instantly felt relieved. Before they established their mask system, disagreements often escalated, but now they give each other space and respect. Their system is a silent pact, a reset button that prevents them from saying things they can't take back. When the air gets heavy, one of them simply says, "mask." It's not a wall; it's breathing room. The word mask may feel like rejection or isolation due to the Covid-19 pandemic, but for this mother-daughter duo it's an act of care. It means I love you enough to step away before I hurt you. They still have a lot of ground to cover, but they are ready for it.

Navigating the Silent Wars:
A Comprehensive Resource Guide

The stories shared in *Mother May I—With All Due Respect* reveal a universal truth: the bond between a mother and daughter is a landscape of both immense beauty and profound complexity. For many, reading these letters will stir long-dormant emotions or highlight areas in their own lives that remain tender and unhealed.

Understanding the "silent wars" is the first step, but navigating the journey toward peace—whether that means reconciliation, healthy boundaries, or self-preservation—often requires support beyond the page. You do not have to navigate these waters alone.

The following National Resource List has been curated to provide you with professional guidance, support communities, and educational tools. I have included a dedicated section of LGBTQ+ Resources for Parents designed to help mothers lead with love and understanding, ensuring that the next generation of daughters feels seen, safe, and celebrated for exactly who they are.

This resource page is designed to be your neutral ground. Whether you are a mother trying to understand why your "help" feels like "control," or a daughter struggling to honor your boundaries without losing your connection, you'll find the tools here to lower the shields.

Let's stop surviving our relationship and start reinventing it, with all due respect.

National Resource List: Healing the Mother-Daughter Bond

Mended Relationships: A non-profit focusing on mother-daughter reconciliation. They offer the "Mother-Daughter Reset," a 10-week coaching program designed to repair fractured bonds and break generational cycles.

Mother-Daughter Relationship Healing | Coaching & Support: Offers guided sessions and practical strategies to help mothers and daughters overcome past hurt and foster deeper emotional connection.

The Mother-Daughter Project: Focuses on creating supportive communities that help mothers nurture their daughters through adolescence and into adulthood.

PEAK (Parents of Estranged Adult Kids): A 501(c)(3) dedicated to helping parents recover from the trauma of estrangement, offering a safe and supportive environment for relational auditing and healing.

I Am My Daughter's Keeper: A national nonprofit that addresses the multigenerational impact of mother-daughter relationships on women across all ethnicities.

PFLAG National: The premier organization for parents and families of LGBTQ+ people. They provide confidential peer support, local chapter meetings, and educational booklets like "Our Daughters and Sons."

Family Equality: A national nonprofit offering trusted information on policies and parenting resources for LGBTQ+ families at every stage of life.

The Trevor Project (For Parents)

Global Support & Crisis Resources

If the "silent war" has escalated into a crisis or if you are seeking professional community support, these organizations provide specialized care.

Psychology Today Directory – Use this global tool to find therapists specializing in family conflict, maternal narcissism, or enmeshment across the USA, UK, and Canada.

Narcissistic Abuse Recovery Center – Offers online support groups and trauma-informed coaching for daughters and mothers navigating toxic dynamics.

Daughters of Narcissistic Mothers (DONM) – A dedicated online hub for women seeking to understand and heal from maternal narcissistic traits.

Co-Dependents Anonymous (CoDA) – Provides free online meetings in multiple languages for those struggling with enmeshment and boundary-setting.

Reaching out for help is not a sign of failure; it is an act of courage. Whether you are a mother seeking to better understand your daughter or a daughter seeking to find her voice, these organizations are here to hold space for you. Take your time exploring them. Healing isn't a race, and there is no "right" way to begin.

Glossary

I want you to be able to name your issue. Below is a small list:

Enmeshment: A relationship dynamic where personal boundaries are blurred, and the mother and daughter's emotions are so intertwined that one cannot be happy if the other is not.

Gaslighting: A form of psychological manipulation where one person makes the other question their own memory, perception, or sanity (e.g., "I never said that, you're being too sensitive").

Parentification (Role Reversal): When a daughter is forced to take on the emotional or practical responsibilities of a parent, often becoming the "mother" to her own mother.

The Mother Wound: The psychological impact of maternal neglect, or the pain passed down through generations of women who were taught to suppress their needs.

Triangulation: When a mother or daughter brings a third person (like a sibling or father) into a conflict to avoid direct communication or to "gang up" on the other.

Momipulation: A term coined by experts to describe the specific guilt-tripping or silencing tactics mothers use when daughters try to assert independence.

Dear mom sorry For
Acting like a Fool and
acting like the ~~Boos~~ Boss
But your the Champ
Around Here Happy BrithDay

In honor of the first letter my daughter ever wrote me as a little girl.